BRIGHT NOTES

THE PELOPONNESIAN WAR BY THUCYDIDES

Intelligent Education

Nashville, Tennessee

BRIGHT NOTES: The Peloponnesian War
www.BrightNotes.com

No part of this publication may be used or reproduced in any manner whatsoever without written permission, except in the case of brief quotations in critical articles and reviews. For permissions, contact Influence Publishers http://www.influencepublishers.com.

ISBN: 978-1-645425-08-3 (Paperback)
ISBN: 978-1-645425-09-0 (eBook)

Published in accordance with the U.S. Copyright Office Orphan Works and Mass Digitization report of the register of copyrights, June 2015.

Originally published by Monarch Press.
Robert Sobel, 1963
2020 Edition published by Influence Publishers.

Interior design by Lapiz Digital Services. Cover Design by Thinkpen Designs.

Printed in the United States of America.

Library of Congress Cataloging-in-Publication Data forthcoming.
Names: Intelligent Education
Title: BRIGHT NOTES: The Peloponnesian War
Subject: STU004000 STUDY AIDS / Book Notes

CONTENTS

1)	Introduction	1
2)	Textual Analysis	5
	Books 1 and 2	5
	Books 3 and 4	18
	Book 5	44
	Book 6	59
	Books 7 and 8	72
3)	Conclusion of the War and Summary	89
4)	Essay Questions and Answers	99
5)	Selected Bibliography	104

INTRODUCTION TO THUCYDIDES

In 493 B.C. the Persian War, one of the most decisive in world history, was begun between the large and powerful Persian Empire and the Greek city states. Had Persia won, it is quite possible that western civilization would never have developed, and in its place, a semi-oriental despotism would have controlled the world. But the Greeks, led by the democratic city-state of Athens, won the war, thus preserving their remarkable civilization, not the least of whose accomplishments was the idea of democracy.

Athens was the leader of the Delian League, an organization formed during the war as a defensive alliance against Persia. The League was not dissolved after the war, for the Greeks feared that Persia might rise up once more. In time, Athens transformed this alliance of equals into a vehicle for her own aggrandizement, in particular using its funds for her own interests. Within a few decades Greece was once more threatened with conquest. Whereas the Persians were foreigners who attempted to conquer Greece and subjugate it to a tyranny, Athens was a fellow member of the civilization, which spoke in terms of sharing its knowledge and accomplishments with less fortunate cities. Nevertheless, this was imperialism, and the other members of the Delian League began to break away from Athens, turning to Sparta, a powerful state which was not a member of the League.

There were many differences between the two states. Athens was Ionian while Sparta was Dorian. These were two separate peoples with differing cultures. (A third group, the Aeolians, included such states as Naupactus, Thebes, and Thermum.) Athens was a democratic sea power, while Sparta was an oligarchic land power. Athenian culture and learning was superior to that of Sparta. The Spartans were conservative in all things, while Athenians were noted for their willingness to take risks. Thus, although they had a common heritage and had fought together against Persia, the two states had long standing differences.

By the middle of the fifth century B.C. Athenian imperialism had reached serious proportions. Potidaea, a colony of the Dorian city of Corinth and an unwilling member of the Athenian empire, refused to allow Athens to interfere in her internal affairs. In addition, Corinth's colony of Corcyra had founded a colony of its own, Epidamnus. When Corinth and Corcyra disputed the status of the colony, Athens took Corcyra's side, further alienating the Corinthians. Finally, Athens issued the Megaran decrees, which ruined the rich carrying trade of the Dorian colony of Megara. These, then, were the underlying and immediate causes of the war.

THUCYDIDES

Although little is known of his early life, it is believed that Thucydides was born sometime between 470 B.C. and 460 B.C. His family was wealthy, owning gold mines on the Thracian coast.

Thucydides' early life went almost unrecorded. It is believed that he studied philosophy under Anaxagoras, a dualist who was later expelled from Athens for his views on religion. There is a story of his having burst into tears of joy on hearing Herodotus, the "father of history," read his works. Later on Herodotus congratulated Olorus, Thucydides' father, on the fine literary taste of the son.

Thucydides was a general in the early part of the Peloponnesian War. He failed to relieve the Athenian forces at Amphipolis in time to prevent their falling to the Spartan commander, Brasidas, and for this was exiled from Athens for twenty years. He went to his family estates in Thrace, and observed the rest of the war from a distance. After the war Thucydides returned to Athens, where he died around 400 B.C.

Thucydides visited almost every theater of the war, and to a great extent relied upon his own observations in his work. In addition, he looked through the documents, spoke to eyewitnesses whenever possible, and verified his material with individuals involved in the conflict. In short, he is considered the first "scientific historian." Some writers believe Thucydides was attempting to do for history what Socrates was doing for philosophy-to view it with rationalistic objectivity.

Thucydides was a Sophist, a member of a group whose beliefs were diametrically opposed to those of Socrates on many issues. He believed that there were no absolute truths and, as the greatest Sophist of them all, Protagoras said, "man is the measure of all things." It was this relativism which led to his attempts at detachment, which in turn resulted in an apparent willingness to criticize Athens, his native city, which he admired. In all probability, his exile (perhaps at the hands of Cleon, who is an "anti-hero" in the book) added to this somewhat.

Like most educated Greeks of his day, Thucydides was strongly interested in and influenced by the drama, and he wrote in a style resembling that of the tragedy. In Greek tragedies the sin of pride (hybris) is followed by an act of folly, and then by punishment (nemesis). Thus, in the *Peloponnesian War*, the Athenians were defeated because of sins committed during the fighting.

In this, we can see that Thucydides had a mechanistic view of history; there is little room for free will in his philosophy. When faced with similar problems, he believed, all men will react in similar ways. Nor does Thucydides believe the gods can interfere in human affairs. Like all Sophists, he did not think that one had to bring in the deities to explain human affairs. As one author wrote, "Properly to appreciate Thucydides, one may contrast the *History of the Peloponnesian War* with the Book of Kings (in the Bible). Each book records how **catastrophe** overwhelmed a city, and each book attempts to explain why. Chronologically, the two books were separated by only about two hundred years, but in attitude they are light-years apart."

Believing as he did that humans act the same in similar circumstances, Thucydides thought his history of the war could be read with profit by future generations, and the lessons of the war could be applied to prevent future conflicts. Thus, Thucydides wrote his book as a lesson in morality as well as a history. As such, it often presents facts as fitted into preconceived patterns, a method which today's historians try to avoid. In addition, he tended to stress political and military events, and almost completely ignored economic and social factors. Still, Thucydides is generally regarded as one of the greatest historians of all times.

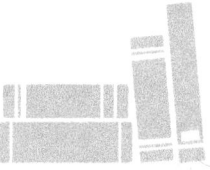

PELOPONNESIAN WAR

TEXTUAL ANALYSIS

BOOKS 1 AND 2

CHAPTER 1

Thucydides tells us that he began to write his book at the beginning of the War, for he knew even then that it would be the most important event in Greek history. In the early period, there was no unity on the peninsula. This came with the Trojan War, in which for the first time the city-states acted together. This War was decided by sea power, which Thucydides believed was the most important source of Greece's strength. After the war, those cities with large armies declined, while those with important navies became more powerful. At this time the old hereditary monarchies began to give way to tyrannies resting on wealth and naval strength.

The city-states unified once more during the Persian Wars, after which two rival blocs appeared. The Athenian group was based on naval power, while the Lacedaemons (Spartans) headed a military confederation. "Athens imposed contributions in money on all but Chios and Lesbos." Conflicts began between the Athenian and Spartan states, and the underlying cause of the conflict was the growth of Athens' power and Sparta's fear of encirclement.

CHAPTER 2

The immediate cause of the war was Athens' attempt to intervene in a conflict between the city-states of Corinth and Corcyra. The Corcyraeans asked Athens for help, and received a defensive alliance from the Athenian Assembly. Since Corinth was allied with Sparta, the groundwork for an Athenian-Spartan war was laid.

Next followed two incidents which heightened tensions. An Athenian-Corcyraean naval force clashed with one from Corinth. Athens said her action was purely defensive, but Corinth claimed it constituted aggression, and broke a truce which formerly had existed.

The second incident involved the Athenian attempt to prevent a revolt of Potidaea. Sparta promised the Potidaeans assistance, and armed with this backing, Potidaea and other states revolted against Athens. The Peloponnesian League, headed by Sparta, sent aid. The Athenians, led by Callias and Phormio, blockaded Potidaea and routed her allies, including Corinth.

CHAPTER 3

Corinth called a meeting of the Peloponnesian League at Sparta to discuss Athenian provocations. The Corinthian envoys speak, telling the Spartans they are too conservative and hesitant. Their isolation prevents them from realizing that dynamic Athens was in the process of taking over all Greece. Athens is weak but acts strong, while Sparta, though strong, behaves as though it were weak. The Athenians, in response to this, observe that their leadership is deserved, due to their actions in the Persian Wars. "That empire we acquired by no violent means, but because you were unwilling to prosecute to its conclusion the war against the barbarian, and because the allies attached themselves to us and spontaneously asked us to assume the command." Then King Archidamus of Sparta expresses his belief that Spartan caution is well advised, and proclaims his opposition to war. But Sthenelaidas, an Ephor, speaks for war, and the assembly follows him rather than the King.

Comment

The following points may be observed.

(1) Thucydides shows the various steps leading to war, showing how one builds upon the other.

(2) The speeches of the Corinthians and Athenians set a pattern which is followed for the rest of the book. Most of the author's ideas are presented in this fashion.

(3) Many historians see a similarity between the background of the Peloponnesian War and World War I. In both cases it is the allies, and not the main powers, which move for war, and in both cases the existence of an expansionist power (Athens and Germany) disturbs the status quo. Thucydides, who believed that history repeated itself, would have appreciated this.

CHAPTER 4

Thucydides begins this chapter by recounting the expansionist activities of Athens after the Persian Wars. The Spartans were disturbed at the construction of a wall around Athens and the growth of Athenian naval power. But Themistocles, the Athenian leader, was able to still their fears. The Athenians fortified their port of Piraeus and constructed a new harbor, both of which acts were viewed with suspicion by other city-states. At the same time the Spartan commander, Pausanias, conducted raids against Cyprus and Byzantium, which struck fear in the hearts of other Greek states. They appealed to Athens for leadership, and were accepted, thus forming the basis for the Athenian empire. During the next few years Athens continued to expand, Spartan mistrust grew, and the allies of each power clashed with the other.

CHAPTER 5

Wishing to discover their chances of success against the Athenians, the Spartans went to Delphi to consult the Oracle, who answered "that if they put their whole strength into the war, victory would be theirs, and the promise that he himself would be with them, whether invoked or uninvoked." Then the Spartans called a second Congress at Lacedaemon and put the question of war or peace before their allies. The Corinthians spoke, urging war due to Athenian provocations, and observing that the strength of the League was such that victory would surely be theirs. Then embassies were sent to Athens "in order to obtain as good a pretext for war as possible." The Spartans tried to turn the Athenians against Pericles, their leader, but failed. Then Thucydides digresses, and tells of the treachery of Pausanias of Sparta and Themistocles of Athens, both of whom die.

In taking up the story once more, Thucydides relates the demands made by Sparta against Athens, which amounted to a breakup of the Athenian empire. Pericles urged the Athenians to refuse all the demands and not yield an inch. If war comes, he said, the Athenians, through their naval power, would be able to take care of themselves easily. He would be willing to free Athens' allies if Sparta would do the same with theirs, and be willing to arbitrate the dispute. Still, Pericles maintains his strong line at the end of his speech. "It must be thoroughly understood that war is a necessity; but that the more ready we accept it, the less will be the ardour of our opponents, and that out of the greatest dangers communities and individuals acquire the greatest glories." The Assembly takes his advice, making war inevitable.

BOOK TWO

CHAPTER 6

When Thebes, an ally of Sparta, attacks Plataea, an ally of Athens, in the Spring of 431 B.C., the war may be said to have begun. The Thebans were repulsed, and prisoners were taken. Athens sent reinforcements to Plataea, and prepared for war. Sparta ordered her allies to build up their military and naval forces. Both sides were eager for war. "Zeal is always at its height at the commencement of an undertaking; and on this particular occasion Peloponnese and Athens were both full of young men whose inexperience made them eager to take up arms, while the rest of Hellas stood straining with excitement at the conflict of its leading cities."

> **Comment**

Thucydides makes two points at the outset of **Book Two**. First, the Theban prisoners were treated with a measure of humanity, and second, both sides were eager for war, viewing it as a sort of game. In later years, the author shows that both attitudes change drastically.

After the Plataean incident, the Spartans organized their allies for an expedition against Athens. Archidamus, leader of the Spartans, made a speech in which he tells his officers of his tactics and strategy.

> **Comment**

At this point, Thucydides reveals his interest in and mastery of military matters. This speech is considered one of the best short statements of Greek military thinking.

The Athenian leader, Pericles-a friend of Archidamus though his foe-organized the Athenian force for the defense. Realizing that the walls of Athens were impregnable, he commanded the people of the outlying districts to gather within the city. Although it was difficult to leave their homes, the citizens listened to Pericles, and Athens was crowded with humanity.

Archidamus then marched on Athens, and was criticized for hesitating before attacking the town of Aenoe. This delay gave the Athenians needed time to organize their defenses. The attack on Aenoe failed, and Archidamus was obliged to bypass it and head for Athens instead. He tried to lure Pericles out of the city in order to engage in open combat, but the Athenians, safe where they were, refused to budge. Instead, a fleet of one hundred ships was sent to ravage the enemy's cities. Thucydides then describes the activities of the fleet, showing how, with Athens under siege, the Athenians were able to seize the advantage in the first years of the fighting. In addition to these attacks, Pericles sent a force to Megara and ravaged the territory of that ally of Sparta.

At this point, Thucydides writes of the funeral of those Athenians who fell in the first clashes of the war. After describing the methods by which the Athenians care for their dead, he has Pericles deliver a funeral oration over their bodies. Pericles' eulogy is the most famous part of the book, and one of the greatest statements as to the meaning of democracy and freedom the world knows.

Pericles begins by apologizing for having the presumption of speaking over the brave dead. He then forgives himself by noting that such was a custom of the city. At first he speaks of the history of Athens, the sources of its greatness and power. All know the history of the city, so Pericles does not go into it in detail. Instead, he analyzes the past to find what made Athens great, so that its citizens can appreciate their heritage and foreigners may copy. "Its administration favors the many instead of the few; that is why it is called a democracy. If we look to the laws, they afford equal justice to all in their private differences; if to social standing, advancement in public life falls to reputation for capacity, class considerations not being allowed to interfere with merit; nor again does poverty bar the way, if a man is able to serve the state, he is not hindered by the obscurity of his condition."

Pericles notes that Athens has no secrets; it is an "open society." He is convinced of the superiority of Athens' ways, and feels that those who come to conquer will stay to learn. "In short, I say that as a city we are the school of Greece."

At this point, Pericles turns to the dead. They gave their lives for freedom, he says, knowing full well what they were dying for. "For it is not the miserable that would most justly be unsparing of their lives; these have nothing to hope for: it is rather they to whom continued life may bring reverses as yet unknown, and to whom a fall, if it came, would be most tremendous in its consequences. And surely, to a man of spirit, the degradation of cowardice must be immeasurably more grievous than the unfelt death which strikes him in the midst of his strength and patriotism!" For these reasons, Pericles does not attempt to console the parents of the dead; their honor is so great that such consolation would be unnecessary.

CHAPTER 7

The funeral ends the first year of the war. With the summer came a new attack from Sparta and her allies. Archidamus, apparently giving up his attempt to take Athens itself, lays the countryside waste.

More deadly than the Spartans, however, was a mysterious plague greater than any in the past. Thucydides thought it came from Egypt, but is not sure. In any case, it hit Piraeus first, and from there spread out to Athens proper. Thucydides describes the symptoms - "violent heats in the head and redness and inflammation in the eyes, the inward parts, such as the throat or tongue, becoming bloody and emitting an unnatural and foul breath."

Comment

The description of the plague does not give us any idea of what it might have been. The symptoms are unlike those of bubonic plague, typhus, smallpox, etc., and this leads many to doubt the accuracy of the description. Thucydides does say that the plague was spread by "the influx from the country into the city," indicating he realized the epidemic nature of disease.

The plague demoralized the Athenians, and lead to a disintegration of national sentiment.

Meanwhile, the Spartan forces continued to advance, taking an area from which Athens mined most of its silver (Laurium). Some Athenians wanted to leave the city and fight the invaders, but Pericles, who was still general, refused to allow them to leave the protection of the walls. Instead, he mounted another naval attack against the enemy's cities. Thus, while Sparta was destroying the Athenian area, the Athenians were laying waste to the Peloponnesian coastline.

The victories overseas did not add to Pericles' popularity. The plague and the Spartan depredations continued to demoralize the Athenians, and they blamed their difficulties on their leaders, especially Pericles. Feeling obliged to defend his course of action, Pericles delivered a speech to the population.

"A man may be personally ever so well off," he said, "and yet if his country be ruined he must be ruined with it; whereas a flourishing commonwealth always affords chances of salvation to unfortunate individuals." He urges the Athenians to seek a greater identification with the city and realize that if it falls, they fall with it. The choice is between "submission with loss of independence and danger with the hope of preserving that independence." Freedom brings dangers and responsibilities, but is well worth the risks. The Athenians are reminded of their greatness, and are urged to remember their past glories in the moment of despair. "For the judgment of mankind is as relentless to the weakness that falls short of a recognized renown, as it is jealous of the arrogance that aspires higher than its due."

Then Pericles reviewed the strategy of the war. Despite all appearances of Spartan victory, the war was going well. Athens was holding fast, and the Spartan homeland was being destroyed. Athens' true possessions lay in its spirit, and not in farms. The farms could be rebuilt, but if the spirit was broken, then Athens would surely be defeated. He urged the Athenians not to send heralds to Sparta to ask for peace, for such a peace would destroy the state.

Pericles convinced the Athenians to continue the war, but many still opposed him. As a result, he was fined. Not long after, however, he was reelected general. Thucydides, a strong supporter of Pericles, writes: "For as long as he was the head of the state during the peace, he pursued a moderate and conservative policy; and in his time its greatness was at its height. When the war broke out, he also seems to have rightly gauged the power of his country." Thucydides writes that Pericles knew the temper of the city, was a politician as well as a statesman, and had the knack of bringing out the best in the Athenian spirit. He intimates that he was the only invaluable man the city had. Pericles died of the plague shortly thereafter, and with his death the city began to stray from his moderate course of action. Pericles was able to maintain the empire, but did not try to enlarge it through conquests. His successors were not so moderate in their approach. This new ruthlessness could be seen when, shortly after Pericles' death, envoys from the Peloponnesian League were put to death.

During the remainder of the summer of 430 B.C., the Athenians continued their naval attacks against the enemy. During the following winter Potidaea, the stanch ally of Sparta, fell to the Athenians under Xenophon, who granted the city a moderate treaty. The Athenians blamed their generals for being too soft, and afterwards settlers were sent to Potidaea to colonize it.

Comment

Thucydides indicates on several occasions that the plague and subsequent death of Pericles was a turning point in the war. Up to then, the Athenians were fighting a defensive war in order to maintain their freedom. Despite cries for blood, Pericles was able to maintain this course. The death of Pericles brought less moral leaders to the fore, as could be seen in the deaths of the Peloponnesian envoys and the reaction to the moderate peace granted Potidaea. As the war continued, the temper of Athens would grow more totalitarian and less democratic.

CHAPTER 8

In the summer of 429 B.C. the Peloponnesians mounted still another attack on Athens, once again being led by Archidamus. He headed in the direction of Plataea, but before he could reach the city, envoys came to meet with the Spartans. Reminding Archidamus of guarantees given them by Sparta after the Persian Wars, they asked to be spared from fighting. Archidamus responded that he would recognize their neutrality, so long as they did not befriend the Athenians. After consultations, the Plataeans replied that their alliance with Athens forbade such a promise. Archidamus then offered to return their farms to them after the war was over. For the time being, he would have to occupy them. If the Plataeans resisted, however, he would have to lay the land waste. After consulting with the Athenians, Plataea decided to resist. After appealing to the gods to witness his good faith, Archidamus began the siege of Plataea.

Comment

The moderate position of Archidamus - who, remember, was a friend and admirer of Pericles though a Spartan - will later be contrasted with the ruthlessness of the Athenians when presented with a similar situation.

Thucydides next describes the fortifications of Plataea in a passage which shows his knowledge of defensive armaments. When the Spartans failed in their move to take the city, they attempted to fire it. Although the conflagration was great, wind and rain combined to save the city. With this, the Spartans inaugurated a blockade of Plataea.

While this was going on, the Athenians, led by Xenophon, marched against the Chalcidians. They met with defeat, and were forced to return to the city. Soon after, the Peloponnesian forces attacked Athens' ally, Acarnania, by land and sea. After some preliminary battles, Phormio arrived with part of the Athenian fleet to aid the Acarnanians. At the battle of Stratus he gave the Peloponnesians a sound beating, which in part compensated for defeat at the hands of The Chalcidians.

As the two sides gathered to renew the battle, the Spartan commander spoke to his men on the question of their position. He said that they were braver than the Athenians, who nonetheless excelled in science. Still, bravery was better than science, and would win the next encounter.

Thucydides then writes of Phormio's speech to his men, in which the Athenian tells them not to fear the numerical superiority of the Spartans. They had defeated the enemy once, and they would do so again. In a speech somewhat reminiscent of those of Pericles, he tells them that their unity and belief in themselves would give them strength against the enemy, which was divided and at odds with one another. Phormio concludes by saying, "And may I remind you once more that you have defeated most of them already; and beaten men do not face a danger twice with the same determination."

Comment

These two speeches are considered models of their type. Each commander stresses his strength, does not underestimate his enemy, and shows abilities in stirring men to battle.

At first the victory goes to the Peloponnesians, who outmaneuver Phormio and destroy a good part of the Athenian fleet. But the Athenians rally, recover, and counterattack, finally sweeping the Peloponnesian fleet from the sea.

During the winter of 429 B.C. the Spartans tried to take Piraeus in a surprise attack. Confusion reigned in Athens; the Piraeans thought that Sparta had taken nearby Salamis, while Athens thought Piraeus had fallen. The next day the Athenians mobilized and sent a force to Piraeus and a fleet to Salamis (site of the famous naval battle of the Persian Wars). The Peloponnesians withdrew, and conditions settled down to normal once more.

For the rest of the year each side made forays against the other, but none were decisive.

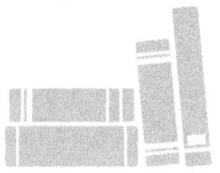

PELOPONNESIAN WAR

TEXTUAL ANALYSIS

BOOKS 3 AND 4

BOOK THREE
CHAPTER 9

Archidamus attacked Athens once more in the summer of 428 B.C. The Peloponnesian force destroyed the area, and then withdrew.

Archidamus' attack moved the citizens of Lesbos to revolt against Athens. Lesbos had wanted to withdraw from the Athenian empire previously, but held back because the Spartans would not offer her protection

Comment

The defection of Lesbos was a serious matter, for Athens feared it might cause other allies to leave the empire. In addition, Lesbos had a powerful fleet which, if added to that of the Peloponnesian states, could negate Athens' superiority on the sea.

When news of Lesbos' disalliance reached Athens, a debate began. It was decided to send a fleet to the city to force it to remain in the empire. Lesbos (which was an island) prepared for the attack, and was ready when it came. When the Athenians demanded they dismantle their fleet and walls, the Mitylenians, whose city was on Lesbos, tried to negotiate a peace. At the same time, however, they continued their preparations for war, sending envoys to Sparta to seek aid. They attacked the Athenian force before reinforcements could be sent, however, and won an initial victory. The Athenians then called upon their allies, and took positions around the city. Meanwhile Asopius, the son of Phormio, led an Athenian naval force in destroying the Mitylenian coastline.

The scene now turns to the Mitylenian envoys sent to the Spartans. The envoys speak, justifying their defection from Athens against those who might accuse them of treason. The Mitylenians say they will speak with "justice and honesty," "because we know that there can never be any solid friendship between individuals, or union between communities that is worth the name, unless the parties be persuaded of each other's honesty, and be generally congenial the one to the other." They had joined with Athens to defeat the Persians, but once that war ended, they began to distrust Athenian expansionist activities. In breaking with Athens, they claim, Mitylene was only acting in self-defense.

Then the envoys speak of their possible value to the Peloponnesian League. Athens is wasted by disease and deficit financing. An all-out Spartan attack would crush the city, if it could be mounted within a few months. The Mitylenians would be willing to join in such an attack, and their power would ensure its success. "Lesbos may appear far off, but when help is wanted she will be found near enough."

The speech convinces the Spartans, and Lesbos is accepted as a full member of the League. In addition, it is decided to launch an all-out attack on Athens, thus following the Mitylenian strategy.

The Athenians, on hearing of this plan, sent out a large fleet to ravage the Peloponnesian area as a show of strength. The Spartan attack plan was shelved temporarily, as Athens took the offensive. In order to punish the defectors, Athens reinforced her garrison around Lesbos and heightened the attack. Then Thucydides describes the fortifications, the attack, and the methods by which the Athenians took the surrounding area.

Meanwhile, the Spartans and their allies were finally able to capture part of Plataea, although most of the citizens of that city were able to escape.

Back in Mitylene, the citizens suffered under the Athenian attack. But her citizens took courage when Salaethus of Sparta slipped through the lines to tell them that help was on its way. During the next summer (427 B.C.) a Spartan fleet, led by Alcidas, set out for Mitylene, and Cleomenes, at the head of a Peloponnesian column, invaded Attica and destroyed everything in sight.

Alcidas took his time in getting to Mitylene, and the city was obliged to surrender to the Athenians, "upon the understanding that the Mitylenians should be allowed to send an embassy to Athens to plead their cause, and that Paches (the Athenian General) should not imprison, make slaves of, or put to death any of the citizens until its return."

Meanwhile, Alcidas arrived at the outskirts of Mitylene at the head of the Peloponnesian fleet. When he learned of the Athenian capture of the city, he and his officers considered what to do. Teutiaplus of Elea suggested a surprise attack, since the Athenians did not as yet know of the fleet.

Alcidas was not impressed with this argument, although many of his officers agreed with Teutiaplus. Others urged him to land in the area and serve as a nucleus for an attack against Athenian allies. This, too, was rejected. Instead, he proceeded along the shore, took prisoners wherever he went, and butchered them.

By then the Athenians had learned of the Peloponnesian fleet, and Alcidas was forced to flee. Fearful that the fleet might land in Ionia and murder its inhabitants, Paches followed Alcidas. As soon as he realized that he had been outdistanced, however, Paches gave up the chase.

On the way back to Mitylene, Paches landed at Notium, which was divided into two rival camps. He settled a dispute between them, and soon after Athenians arrived in the area to colonize it. Then Paches returned to Mitylene, where he awaited the return of the envoys to Athens.

The Athenians greeted the Mitylenian envoys by putting one of their number, a Spartan, to death. Then the Assembly debated the question of what to do with the captured city. Some suggested that the entire male population be killed and the women and children be made slaves. Since Mitylene had revolted against Athens without cause, this was considered a fair treatment. Accordingly, a galley was sent to Paches with that order.

On the following day many Athenians repented their harsh judgment. The Mitylenian envoys, on seeing this, moved that the question of their city's fate be put to a vote. The Assembly was recalled, and the debate began.

Comment

The ensuing debate is the heart of this book. An entire city was to be destroyed due to the revolt of a few. Many Athenians realize the unfairness of this, and in addition, fear the brutalizing effect of such a sentence upon Athens herself. Others, arguing that a nation must be tough in wartime, urge Mitylene's destruction. The debate, then, was between those who wished to preserve Athenian freedom in time of war, and those who thought that it would have to be shelved while the fighting was on.

The debate is opened with a speech by Cleon, who Thucydides describes as "the most violent man at Athens."

Comment

The ideas and speeches of Cleon were essentially of a rabble-rousing sort, and offer an example of what happens when a democracy resorts to mob rule and forgets its essential basis. Earlier in the work, Pericles upheld the Athenian Constitution against those who would substitute for it majority rule. Now Cleon begins his campaign to replace the Constitution by voice votes of the Assembly.

Cleon begins by saying, "I have often before now been convinced that a democracy is incapable of empire, and never more so than by your present change of mind in the matter of Mitylene." He implies and later states that he would gladly choose a strong Athenian empire over a strong Athenian democracy. The Mitylenians revolted, and must be made to suffer, both for their sins and as an example to those who might think of revolt in the future. "Your empire is a despotism," and not a democracy. One may be able to maintain democracy at home and yet forget about it in dealings with foreign states. Such must be the course of Athens. He then implies that those who disagree with him in this are traitors.

Comment

Some see a similarity between Cleon's approach and that of the late Sen. McCarthy in this kind of an argument, and argue that if Thucydides is correct - and nations undergo similar developments-perhaps America is losing her democracy today in a manner similar to that in which Athens lost hers.

Cleon then outlines Mitylene's crimes, and asks for her destruction. What would happen if the roles were reversed? Would Athens receive mercy from her conquerors? Destroy your enemy, he says, before he can destroy you, and any means employed are good so long as they work. If the Athenians are unwilling to act in this fashion, Cleon suggests they give up their empire, for no one will either respect or trust them in the future. "Punish them as they deserve, and teach your other allies by a striking example that the penalty of rebellion is death."

The next speaker is Diodotus, who favors mercy. "I think the two things most opposed to good counsel are haste and passion." He then attacks Cleon by observing that only through careful counsel can a reasonable judgment be arrived at. If Athens acts through fear, the internal order and the value structure of the city would be destroyed as surely as if Sparta took the city. In addition, Cleon misuses oratory, which in Athens is supposed to inform and analyze, and not inflame men's minds.

Diodotus admits that Mitylene is guilty of crimes, but "the question before us as sensible men is not their guilt, but our interests." Severe punishment is no deterrent to further crimes. Next follows an impassioned plea which today is used as an argument against capital punishment.

Comment

In attacking Cleon, Diodotus does not refer to the Athenian Constitution, but rather as to what would serve the city best. Unlike Pericles, Diodotus is not an effective spokesman for lasting values. He implies that if the destruction of Mitylene would aid the Athenian cause, he would willingly accept it.

If the punishment is carried out, Diodotus concludes, the pro-Athenian groups in other cities would be alienated. "Good policy against an adversary is superior to the blind attacks of brute force."

A vote was then taken on the question, and Diodotus' forces won by a narrow margin. A galley was quickly sent to stop the first ship before it reached Mitylene and told Paches of the early decision to destroy the city. The second ship arrived in the nick of time, and the decree was not carried out.

Cleon's followers did win a victory, however. Some Mitylenian ambassadors were executed. Mitylene's walls were leveled, and her ships confiscated. In addition, much of her territory was taken and distributed to Athenians.

| CHAPTER 10

During the next summer, an Athenian force under Nicias went to the island of Minoa, which had been used as a fortified post by Sparta's ally, Megara. The island was taken after a brief skirmish.

Meanwhile, the Spartans completed their capture of Plataea. The Peloponnesian commander offered an honorable surrender, promising to punish only the Plataean leaders, and extend fair hearings to all accused. Plataea surrendered on these terms, and at first the Spartans indicated their willingness to follow their promises. At the hearings, Astymachus and Lacon, two Plataean leaders spoke for their city.

The leaders began by reminding the Spartans of their premises. They fear that they will not be kept. The Spartan attempts to equate neutrality and indirect aid to Athens with guilt is not fair. The past record of the city - the Plataeans fought well in the Persian Wars - is recalled. During an earthquake in Sparta, Plataeans were sent to that city to aid the survivors. Plataea did not want to enter into an alliance with Athens, but was forced to do so when Sparta aided Thebes, the enemy of Plataea. Thebes had been guilty of treason during the Persian Wars, and did not deserve assistance from Sparta.

The Plataeans add that Sparta has a record of fair dealings. If her pledge to the defeated city is broken, she will no longer be trusted by any other Greek state. The Plataeans close with an appeal for mercy.

A reply to the appeal is given by the Theban allies of Sparta. They say that Thebes would not speak at all were it not for the fact that misrepresentations had been made by the Plataeans. Their quarrel with Plataea was based on the unwillingness of Plataea to cooperate in some ventures which would have aided both sides. It is true that Plataea did not cooperate with the Persians, but the city's resistance was based on Athenian support for its position. This was not bravery, but caution. Thebes was as anti-Persian as Plataea, but the Theban leaders, who then were not representative of the people, submitted to the invaders. After the war, Thebes led the resistance to Athenian imperialism, while the Plataeans submitted without a struggle.

As to the Plataean charge that her alliance with Athens was entered into for defensive reasons, the Thebans ask why Plataea attacked cities which did not menace her. Once more, Plataea was serving her selfish interest, and not the cause of Greece. "When the Athenians took the path of injustice you followed them."

Finally, the Thebans attempt the justify their aggressions against Plataea. At first the Plataeans welcomed Thebes; the charges of attack came later on. Thebes' intentions toward Plataea were not hostile, and if the Plataeans desired to interpret them as aggression, it was their problem, and not that of Thebes.

The Spartan judges consider the matter, and in a short time come out with a judgment against Plataea. Thucydides indicated that this was done to ensure Theban support in the future, and not due to Plataean guilt. The city is then razed, and its inhabitants killed.

Comment

Thucydides contrasts the fates of Mitylene and Plataea, showing the effects of Athenian democratic sentiments in saving the former and Spartan lack of morality in destroying the latter.

Meanwhile, the Peloponnesian fleet, led by Alcidas, was caught in a storm. Alcidas reorganized the force and set out for Corcyra, where a revolution had broken out. The rest of this chapter deals with the Corcyraean revolt.

There were two factions contending in the city: one which favored alliance with Athens, the other with Corinth. A conference was held, and it was agreed that the Athenian alliance would remain, but Corcyra would try to be friends of the Peloponnesians at the same time. But Peithias, a friend of Athens, was assassinated along with sixty of his followers, and open fighting began between the democratic (pro-Athenian) and oligarchic (pro-Spartan) forces.

The oligarchic party summoned an assembly, and claimed to have saved the city from being enslaved by Athens. They suggested an almost complete isolation of Corcyra as their method of keeping neutral. The motion was accepted, and Athens was notified.

The Athenians arrested the Corcyraean envoys, who they viewed as revolutionaries. Meanwhile, a Spartan force landed near Corcyra and was destroyed by members of the democratic party. Both forces then looked for allies to use against the other in the civil war.

The democrats gained more allies, especially among the slaves, than the oligarchic forces. They proceeded to win several victories and consolidate past gains. The Athenians arrived, and attempted to mediate the dispute. Then they indicated a desire to leave, but were delayed by the democrats, who wanted their support. The matter was resolved when a Peloponnesian fleet arrived to threaten the city. A battle followed, during which the Corcyraeans and Athenians, in great confusion, were at first disunited. A Peloponnesian victory resulted, and many Corcyraean ships were captured. The Peloponnesians did not follow up their success by taking Corcyra, however, and the democrats, backed by the Athenians, conducted a reign of terror against the oligarchic party, killing many.

The Corcyraean revolt then spread to other cities, which were split between democratic pro-Athenian and oligarchic pro-Spartan factions.

Comment

Thucydides believed that these civil wars were brought on by the Peloponnesian War. Neither side would have dared attack the other were it not for the fact that each was able to call on the services of powerful allies.

The civil wars brought out all the base instincts in man. "In peace and prosperity states and individuals have better sentiments...but war takes away the easy supply of daily wants, and so proves a rough master, that brings most men's characters to a level with their fortunes." "Frantic violence became the attribute of manliness," writes Thucydides.

Comment

In this section, the author analyzes the nature of revolution, those qualities necessary for a successful plotter and leader, and the course of revolts. This is in line with his belief that war destroys morality and honor. Almost two thousand years later Machiavelli, the leading political writer of the Italian Renaissance, would write in a similar manner in *The Prince*.

Where Thucydides decried the wars, however, Machiavelli tended to applaud them.

Thucydides notes that the excesses of the Corcyraean revolt marked the beginning of excesses on both sides. They were "examples of the reprisals exacted by the governed who had never experienced equitable treatment or indeed aught but violence and insolence from their rulers."

Toward the end of that summer (427 B.C.) an Athenian fleet under Laches and Charoeades was sent to Sicily, where the Syracusans and Leontines were at war. The allies of the Leontines called upon Athens for aid, which was given.

CHAPTER 11

During the following winter the plague reappeared in Athens. Over four thousand infantrymen died of it, and the plague inflicted more hardships than any losses to the Peloponnesian forces. In addition, earthquakes in Athens and the surrounding area caused great suffering.

A new invasion against Athens was launched the following summer, this one led by Archidamus' son, Agis. The Peloponnesian force was obliged to turn back, however, due to earthquake activity.

Meanwhile, the Athenians were engaged in battles in Sicily. Charoeades was killed, leaving Laches in sole command. Despite an enemy ambush, the Athenians won the day, taking many prisoners.

Demosthenes led an army against Melos that summer, when that city refused to become part of the Athenian alliance.

Comment

In this way, Thucydides introduces the most significant section of his work: that which dealt with Athens' treatment of Melos.

While Demosthenes was attacking Melos, the Spartans attempted to colonize Heracles, which would be used as a jumping-off place for future attacks against Athens. The Athenians were annoyed, but the colony was not a major threat at the time. Athens countered this move with an effort against the Peloponnesian region.

Meanwhile, Demosthenes was persuaded by the Messenians to attack their enemy, Aetolia, which was almost defenseless. Demosthenes agreed to their plan in order to please the Messenians and also to force nearby states to join with Athens. At first, he met with nothing but success, but then the Aetolians counterattacked and stopped the Athenian army. A second Aetolian attack sent the Athenians flying, and forced them to seek a truce, which was granted. Then Aetolian envoys in Sparta obtained that city's agreement to attack Naupactus, an ancient enemy which had invited the Athenian attack. Eurylochus marched at the head of the Peloponnesian force, which was soon not far from that of Demosthenes. The Athenians moved to save Naupactus, and were successful.

Athenian soldiers took Delos, and proceeded to "purify" it. All those who were about to die, and mothers ready to bear children, would have to do so elsewhere. Then the Athenians celebrated the ancient Delian Games.

Next, Thucydides describes the battle between the Athenians under Demosthenes and the Peloponnesian force commanded by Eurylochus. The Spartan commander was killed as Demosthenes carried the day. Other battles followed, closing the sixth year of the war.

BOOK FOUR

CHAPTER 12

The next summer (425 B.C.), Syracuse and her allies sailed to Messina and occupied the town on the invitation of its inhabitants. Messina revolted against Athens, perhaps because of Athens' inability to defeat Aetolia. Thus, the Peloponnesians won another ally to their cause.

At the same time Agis, son of Archidamus, the Spartan King, invaded Attica and laid waste to the area around Athens. Several Athenian forces moved to attack both the Peloponnesian area and Sicily, where Syracuse and Messina waited for the assault.

The Athenian fleet landed at Pylos, which was about forty-five miles from Sparta. Leaving a force there, the rest of the fleet headed toward Corcyra to put down an uprising, and Sicily. The Spartans, on learning of the taking of Pylos, were at first content to let things rest. Later on, however, a Spartan force was formed to move against the Athenian occupiers, who were led by Demosthenes. The Athenian fortified the area, and then spoke to his men.

Demosthenes urges his men to be valorous and forceful. "In emergencies like ours calculation is out of place. The sooner the danger is faced, the better." He reviews the terrain, and tells his men that the lay of the land is in their favor. Although the Spartans have larger forces at their command, they will be unable to get them to the city, so the battle will be equal.

Demosthenes proved correct in his assessment of the situation. Although the Spartans attacked by land and sea, they were thrown back. The Athenian fleet cut off the Spartans from their sea arm, and in a series of moves defeated them, taking many prisoners.

When the Spartans learned of the defeat at Pylos, they called a meeting and decided to ask for an armistice in that war zone as a prelude for arranging the return of their soldiers.

The Athenians then put forth their terms. The Spartans had to send a portion of food and wine for each man held captive. While the material was being sent, the Athenians promised not to attack Spartan emplacements.

At this point the Spartan envoys spoke before the Athenian assembly.

The Spartans begin their speech in a conciliatory manner. "We beg you to take what we may say, not in a hostile spirit, nor as though we thought you ignorant and wished to lecture you, but rather as a suggestion on the best course to be taken, addressed to intelligent judges." If the Athenians wish, they can press their advantage and gain great success, but if they are in a similar position as the Spartans in the future, what can they expect from their captives? Moderate treatment at this time will bring moderate treatment from the Spartans in the future. "Sensible men are prudent enough to treat their gains as precarious." The Spartans agree that Athens has the advantage, and therefore they are willing to conclude a peace treaty, provided the terms are honorable. "Indeed, if great enmities are ever to be really settled, we think it will be, not by the system of revenge and military success, and by forcing an opponent to swear to a treaty to his disadvantage, but when the more fortunate combatant waives these his privileges, to be guided by gentler feelings, conquers his rival in generosity, and accords peace on more moderate conditions than he expected."

Comment

The popularity of Thucydides rests less on his ability to chronicle the war, than on his observations regarding the nature of man and his institutions. Nowhere is this more clearly demonstrated than in this speech. Great leaders of the Christian period who have read this passage have remarked on this, and on applying his dicta, have often succeeded. Charles II of England, for example, loved Thucydides, and granted an easy peace on his return to England after the English Civil War. As a result, his reign was a happy one. At least one American President, Woodrow Wilson, was a student of this work, which he read on the eve of the treaty making at Versailles after World War I, and it may have affected his attitude at the conferences. Although there is no evidence that Lincoln read the *Peloponnesian War*, certainly his attitude toward the South indicates a strong understanding of the point Thucydides makes.

The Athenians rejected the offer. Led by Cleon (who, as you will remember, supported the "hard line" in the war), they insisted on pressing their advantage. A truce would be granted, they said, but only on terms which resembled unconditional surrender. When the Spartans asked for time to consider the offer, Cleon assailed them, implying that their motives were dishonorable. At this, the envoys returned to Sparta. Their arrival home put an end to the truce, and Sparta asked for the return of her ships, which had been taken by Athens as part of the truce arrangement. Athens charged that Sparta had contravened the truce, and refused to give them back in a singular act of bad faith. With this, the battles at Pylos resumed.

Meanwhile, Syracuse carried on the campaign near Athens' former ally, Messina. Seeing that Athens had only a small naval force in the area, they tried a sea strike, with success. Later on the Athenians were defeated in land battles.

Back at Pylos, the Athenians continued their siege of the city. The attackers suffered from lack of provisions, while Pylos had a stream and was supplied with food by Spartan volunteers. Some Athenians began to wish they had accepted the offer of peace, and Cleon was in disfavor in some circles. He retaliated by accusing Athens' generals of cowardice and incompetence, stating that had he been in command, he would have taken the island.

"Nicias (the Athenian General), hearing the Athenians murmuring against Cleon for not sailing himself if conquest seemed so easy, and further seeing himself the object of attack, told Cleon that for all the generals cared, he might take what force he chose and make the attempt." At first, Cleon thought Nicias was bluffing in his offer to resign the command to him. But then Nicias repeated the offer, and although he shrank from the command, Cleon was obliged to take it. Now he would have to back his strong and irresponsible words with deeds! Cleon then boasted that he would either defeat the Spartans in twenty days or kill them on the spot. Thucydides writes that sensible Athenians rejoiced. If Cleon were successful, they would have won the war. If not, at least Cleon would be out of the way.

Cleon chose Demosthenes as his colleague in the attack, and set out for Pylos. With this, Thucydides launches into a description of the Athenian plan of attack, the lay of the land, etc. The Athenians attacked, and were successful in pushing back the Spartan infantry. Sparta's prestige suffered an irreparable blow, and Cleon was at his height of popularity. He refused to sign a peace and continued to press his advantage. Fearing revolution at home and further losses in the field, the Spartans sent representatives to Cleon to ask for peace. "The Athenians, however, kept grasping at more, and dismissed envoy after envoy without their having effected anything. Such was the history of the affair of Pylos."

CHAPTER 13

The same summer (425 B.C.) the Athenians made an expedition against Corinth, accompanied by the Milesians, Andrians, and Carystians, and under the command of Nicias. Although the defenders made a brave attempt at holding their position, they were defeated in the end. Two hundred and twelve Corinthians and fifty Athenians were killed in the battle.

Comment

Almost alone of all the Greek historians, Thucydides does not exaggerate his figures. In contrast, Herodotus speaks of "millions of Persians" attacking Greece in the Persian campaigns, when actually the figure must have been closer to thousands.

While this was going on, an Athenian force landed at Corcyra, and joined with them in an attack on their enemies. They achieved victory, after which Corcyraeans massacred their foes in an act of great brutality. This ended the Corcyraeans revolution, and also marked a new low in the inhumanity of the war.

The rest of the year was rather quiet, the major occurrence being the destruction of the wall around Chios at the command of Athens.

Early in the following winter, the Mitylenian exiles (see **chapter 9**) regrouped and took some prominent points, from which they planned to retake their city.

Meanwhile Nicias, at the head of an Athenian-Milesian force, prepared to attack Cythera, a Peloponnesian ally. First he took Scandea and Malea, two outlying towns, and then the attack was mounted against Cythera itself. "The Cytherians held their ground for some little while, and then turned and fled into the upper town, where they soon afterward capitulated to Nicias and his colleagues, agreeing to leave their fate to the decision of the Athenians, their lives alone being safe."

The defeat of Cythera sent Sparta into a deep depression. All hopes of winning the war seemed to have vanished. "Accordingly they now allowed the Athenians to ravage their seaboard, without making any movement, the garrisons in whose neighborhoods the descents were made always thinking their numbers insufficient and sharing the general feeling." With this, the Athenians proceeded to win several significant points.

The citizens of Camarina and Gela in Sicily made an armistice that summer, and ambassadors from other cities met with them at Gela in an attempt to bring about a general peace in the area. Hermocrates of Syracuse addressed the gathering.

"If I now address you, Sicilians," he began, "it is not because my city is the least in Sicily or the greatest sufferer by the war, but in order to state publicly what appears to me to be the best policy for the whole island." War, he says, is evil; no one will deny that. All present know why they went to war, and they should ask themselves whether their hopes, if realized, would be worth the general destruction of the entire island of Sicily. Athenian ambition menaces all, and all must unite against it.

Hermocrates does not blame Athens for her ambitions, for her size and wealth have led her to them. Still, must Sicilians go along with her in her madness? Hermocrates' answer is armed neutrality against all, especially Athens, in the struggles.

The Sicilians took his advice, and ended the war among themselves. Athens was informed of the decision, and agreed to accept it. Shortly thereafter, the Athenian fleet sailed away. The fleet received a cold reception in Athens, however. The victories of the past few months had convinced the citizens of the city that no force could withstand them, and the admirals were fined and banished for having left Sicily without subduing it.

During the same summer some citizens of Megara, tiring of the war, decided to ask Athens for peace. The leaders of the city, fearing a loss of their power, told the Athenian generals, Hippocrates and Demosthenes, of this plan, and together they hatched a plan to subdue the city through an Athenian takeover. The long walls of the city were taken with little difficulty, and the city was conquered.

Brasidas, the Peloponnesian commander in the area, learned of the takeover, and took a force to Megara in an attempt to foil the Athenians. A skirmish followed between Boeotian forces and those of Athens before the town, which ended in a draw. Soon after, both the Peloponnesians and the Athenians withdrew from the area.

CHAPTER 14

This book opens with the attempts on the part of Demosthenes to encourage a democratic revolution in Boeotia. If it succeeded, the city might leave the Peloponnesian League and join with

Athens. He arranged for a takeover by Boeotian rebels, while an Athenian force under Hippocrates waited for the proper moment to come to their aid.

About the same time, Brasidas set out for Thrace, marching through Thessaly. He tried to gain the confidence of the Thessalians by telling them that he was trying to destroy Athens, and had no desire to enter into a quarrel with them. He did not want their aid, but asked that they allow him to go through their territory. This was accepted, and Brasidas continued on his way. He soon came to Chalcidice and Dium, which feared Athenian power and welcomed the Peloponnesian force.

Brasidas and Perdiccas, a ruler of Thessaly, disagreed as to what to do about Arrhabaeus, ruler of a neighboring town. Brasidas wanted to offer an alliance to Arrhabaeus, while Perdiccas wanted the Spartan to mind his own business. Nevertheless, Brasidas spoke with Arrhabaeus, disregarding his ally's wishes. Perdiccas responded by withdrawing some of his men from the joint army.

That summer (424 B.C.) Brasidas, together with some Chalcidians, marched against the Andrian colony of Acanthus. The inhabitants of the colony were divided as to their attitude toward the Spartans. Brasidas received permission to speak to the citizens before they made up their minds on the issue.

Brasidas begins by telling the Acanthians that he was sent by Sparta to free Greece from Athenian tyranny. At first Sparta thought she could do this alone, but now she needs allies in the venture. Brasidas is astonished to find such a cool welcome at Acanthus. The army had gone through grave dangers in order to come to them. "It will be a terrible thing if after this you have other intentions, and mean to stand in the way of your own and

Hellenic freedom. It is not merely that you oppose me yourselves; but wherever I go people will be less inclined to join me, on the score that you, to whom I first came - an important town like Acanthus, and prudent men like the Acanthians - refused to admit me." How will he be able to prove to others that his motives are pure? In addition, will other towns believe that the Spartans are able to defend them after such a rebuke? The army is strong, said Brasidas, as seen in the fact that a larger Athenian force did not attack it shortly before, although the two armies were close by each other. Brasidas then promises that he has no desire to limit their freedom in any way. In addition, he will not interfere in the warfare between two factions then going on in Acanthus. If his offer is refused, however, Brasidas will have no alternative to destroying Acanthus. "Endeavor, therefore, to decide wisely, and strive to begin the work of liberation for the Hellenes, and lay up for yourselves endless renown, while you escape private loss, and cover yourselves and your commonwealth with glory."

Brasidas won his point; Acanthus decided to leave the Athenian alliance and join with Sparta, and was joined by other states. Thus, the Athenian successes in Boeotia is balanced by a Spartan victory in Thessaly.

The Athenians next moved to consolidate their gains in Boeotia. An army under Hippocrates and Demosthenes landed in the area and began to advance. The battle between the anti-Athenian Boeotians and the invaders was to take place in Delium, the sanctuary of Apollo. Boeotia fortified the area, after which their commander, Pagondas spoke to them.

First Pagondas defends his choice of an area for the battle. Then, he speaks of the necessity of the Boeotians to defend their homes against the Athenian invaders, and to consider Delium, far from their residences, as an extension of them. The

Athenians "usually march confidently against those who keep still, and only defend themselves in their own country, but think twice before they grapple with those who meet them outside their frontier and strike the first blow if opportunity offers."

Comment

Thus, the now familiar argument that the best defense is an attack.

Pagondas thus persuaded the Boeotians to attack first, and they march to meet the enemy. Before the battle was to begin, Hippocrates addressed the Athenian army. His words will be few, says Hippocrates, for brave men need but few words. Boeotia must be defeated, he says, for Sparta will never invade Athens without the support of the Boeotian cavalry. If Boeotia is defeated there, the Athenians will be spared the trouble of fighting them at home.

Comment

In this way, Hippocrates uses arguments similar to those of Pagondas. He too believes the best defense is an attack.

Before the speech could be concluded, the Boeotians attacked. After a quick skirmish, during which the Athenians almost break through the Boeotian ranks, Pagondas revives his forces and wins the battle.

The Athenians sent envoys asking for the bodies of their dead. The Boeotians refused to return them until the Athenians evacuated the temple of Apollo, which they still held. A series of recriminations followed, during which both sides accused the other of serious breaches of the customs of war.

The Boeotians then attack the Athenians once more, this time using a device which resembled a crude flamethrower. They take the fortress of Delium, after which the Boeotians return the Athenian dead. Although five hundred Boeotians were killed, twice that number of Athenians fell, including Hippocrates.

During that winter Brasidas, having consolidated his gains in Thessaly, moved against the Athenian colony of Amphipolis. With the aid of several snowstorms, Brasidas was able to take the city by surprise, and capture many of those who had not yet fled behind its walls. At this point, Thucydides introduces himself as a leading figure in the war. He was then at the island of Thasos, half a day from Amphipolis. He set out at once for the city, but arrived too late, as Amphipolis had already accepted Brasidas' moderate terms of peace.

The news of the fall of Amphipolis caused great alarm in Athens. "Not only was the town valuable for the timber it afforded for shipbuilding, and the money that it brought in; but also, although the escort of the Thessalians gave the Spartans a means of reaching the allies of Athens as far as the Strymon, yet as long as they were not masters of the bridge but were watched on the side of Eion by the Athenian galleys, and on the land side impeded by a large and extensive lake formed by the waters of the river, it was impossible for them to go any further." Now, the path to Athens lay open. Athenians also feared that Brasidas' moderate terms might encourage other allies to leave the war; his declarations of a desire to free Greece apparently were having their effects. Some towns had already approached him with requests for terms. Because of this, Athens sent emissaries and small forces to many of her allies.

During the same winter the Megarans retook that portion of their city which had been conquered by Athens, and Brasidas marched against Acte, where he won several converts to the Spartan cause.

At this point, Brasidas marched toward Torone, an Athenian ally in Chalcidice. Once more he completed a successful surprise attack, and aided by traitors within Torone, he captured the city. Remembering the success he had with moderate terms at Acanthus, he offered the same to the Toronaeans. Then, he engaged in another battle with the Athenians and again defeated them.

A truce was agreed upon in the spring of 423 B.C. While the conference was on, however, Scione revolted against Athens and went over to Brasidas. A dispute then arose as to the status of the city, in light of the truce. Other towns revolted, including Mende, which Brasidas had taken from the Athenian alliance. The Spartans had problems too, for Illyria betrayed her and joined the Athenian camp. Brasidas marched against the Illyrians and their allies and, before the battle, spoke to his men.

The enemy had more men than he, admits Brasidas, but Spartan bravery once more will carry the day. In addition, the enemy is disorganized and undisciplined, and this too will work in Sparta's favor.

Brasidas lost the ensuing battle, but his retreat was orderly and well-executed. The Athenians retook Mende and now, under the command of Nicias, marched against Chalcidice, which was still in Spartan hands. In addition, Scione was laid waste by Nicias. On seeing the tide turn, Perdiccas left Brasidas and rejoined the Athenian alliance.

Brasidas meanwhile attempted to take Potidaea in a surprise attack, which failed. "So ended the winter and the ninth year of this war of which Thucydides is the historian."

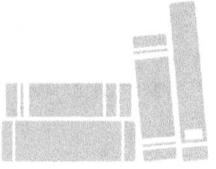

PELOPONNESIAN WAR

TEXTUAL ANALYSIS

BOOK 5

CHAPTER 15

The truce ended in the summer of 422 B.C. and the fighting began once more.

Cleon asked the Athenians to permit him to lead an expedition against Thrace, on the way to which he would visit those towns retaken by Athens the previous year. Permission was granted, and Cleon set out, his first step being Chalcidice.

Cleon took Torone, forcing Brasidas to withdraw, and then set out for Amphipolis.

At about the same time an Athenian envoy, Phaeax, set sail for Italy and Sicily. The Leontines had instituted reforms, and had invited the Syracusans (Sparta's ally) to the city. Phaeax' mission was to convince the Sicilians that the Syracuse alliance would do them no good. He succeeded at Camarina and Agrigentum, but after being spurned at Gela, returned to Athens.

Phaeax stopped at some Italian cities on the way home, speaking with their leaders of friendship with Athens. He met some enemies of his city, but no clashes tool place.

Meanwhile, Cleon based himself at Eion and, after an unsuccessful attempt to take Stagirus, captured Galepsus, a colony of Sparta's ally Thasos. He then sent envoys to Perdiccas and other wishy-washy leaders, and demanded assistance. Brasidas learned of this, and took a position so as to prevent the movement of Cleon's army. He felt that despite the inferior Athenian force, the brash Cleon would attempt to take Amphipolis.

Brasidas' tactics worked. "After remaining quiet for some time, Cleon was at length obliged to do as Brasidas expected. His soldiers, tired of their inactivity, began also seriously to reflect on the weakness and incompetence of their commander and the skill and valor that would be opposed to him, and on their own original unwillingness to accompany him. These murmurs coming to the ears of Cleon, he resolved not to disgust the army by keeping it in the same place, and broke up his camp and advanced." Cleon was brash, and expected no major difficulties in the taking of Amphipolis.

As soon as Brasidas saw this, he moved his force into the city, and awaited the Athenian attack. He had more troops than Cleon, but the Athenian force represented the flower of that city's youth. After showing the Athenians how many men he had, Brasidas resolved to attempt once more the stratagem of a surprise attack which had worked so well in the past. Before leading the charge, he spoke to his men.

Brasidas begins by reminding his men that they are Dorians and the enemy, Ionians; Dorians are accustomed to defeating Ionians, and therefore they should have no trouble. Cleon is overconfident, and this will cause him to lose the battle. "The most successful soldier will always be the man who most happily detects a blunder like this, and who carefully consulting his own means makes his attack not so much by open and regular approaches, as by seizing the opportunity of the moment; and by these stratagems, which do the greatest service to our friends and most completely deceiving our enemies, have the most brilliant name in war." The surprise attack will throw terror into the Athenians, and they won't have a chance.

But Cleon noticed the preparations, and all seemed lost for Brasidas. But Cleon sounded a retreat, preferring to await the coming of reserves before engaging in battle. Before this could be done, however, Brasidas attacked, killed Cleon, and all but completely destroyed the Athenian force. There was a major loss for Sparta, however, as Brasidas himself died in the battle. He was buried with full honors, and Amphipolis considered him one of the founders of the city.

Meanwhile, three Spartans-Ramphias, Autocharides, and Epicydidas-led an army to Thrace. The army reached Thessaly, where it was stopped. On learning that Brasidas had died, they returned home, "themselves not equal to the execution of Brasidas' designs." In addition, the Spartans desired peace, and they had no intention of making moves which might make an armistice impossible.

Both sides wanted an armistice after the battle of Amphipolis. Athens no longer had confidence in her strength, and in addition feared revolts on the part of her allies. The Spartans, realizing that their plan to wreck Athens by devastating the countryside had failed, also desired an end to the fighting. Neither side had realized when the war began what devastation it could bring. The deaths of Cleon and Brasidas, each of whom represented the war parties in their respective cities, made peace easier to take. The foremost candidates for power in each city-Pleistoanax in Sparta and Nicias in Athens-wanted to end the war.

As a result, conferences between the two cities were begun in 422 B.C. Despite some misgivings on the part of allies, the armistice was accepted by both sides soon thereafter. In addition, Sparta and Athens agreed to a fifty year alliance.

Comment

Note that the differences between the two sides had not been resolved. Sparta and Athens wanted a truce, not a peace, so as to prepare for the next round in the fighting.

CHAPTER 16

The peace was unreal, for Sparta's allies were not willing to accept it, and Athens did not trust her enemy. As a result each side violated the truce, although neither Athens nor Sparta themselves were invaded for almost seven years.

Corinthian allies went to Argos, and spoke of Sparta's supposed designs on her allies. Corinth proposed an Argive Confederacy as the best means of preserving the independence of the allies. The Argives were responsive, and passed a decree empowering a body to negotiate with any Hellenic state which wished to join the alliance, with the exception of Sparta and Athens.

Comment

With Athens and Sparta in the process of recovery, Argos, scarcely touched by the war, thus prepared to assume dominance in Greece.

The Mantineans and their allies were the first to join, doing so in fear of Sparta. Upon this, the rest of the Peloponnesian area began to talk of leaving Sparta.

Sparta realized that Corinth was behind the new Confederacy, and sent envoys to that city to prevent her from joining it. Corinth was warned that by so acting, she was breaking the truce and the Spartan alliance. After offering some lame excuse, Corinth rejected the Spartan envoys. Soon after, the Chalcidians and others joined the Argive Confederacy, while Boeotia and Megara remained quiet.

At about the same time, Athens reduced Scione, put the adult males to death, enslaved the others, and occupied the land. The Phocians and Locrians commenced hostilities, and Corinth and the Argives tried to bring Tegea into the Confederacy. Thus, the treaty did not bring an end to war or diplomatic maneuvering.

Spartans invaded Arcadia in the summer of 421 B.C., led by Pleistoanax. Their object was to destroy an enemy faction in Parrhasia. They succeeded in this, and returned home.

Meanwhile, the troops which had gone out with Brasidas returned to Sparta, and were given many benefits.

The meetings between Athenians and Spartans regarding the carrying out of the treaty continued. Sparta had not rebuilt Amphipolis, as was promised, and had failed to persuade her allies to accept the treaty. The Spartan delays raised doubts in Athenian hearts, and mistrust grew. Sparta made attempts to carry out these provisions, but generally was unsuccessful. The Athenians, on their part, also failed to carry out parts of the treaty. Thus, mutual suspicions grew, even while peace reigned.

Meanwhile, a war party gained prominence in Sparta. Cleobulus and Xenares communicated with the Boeotians and Corinthians, and tried to persuade them to bring the Argive group into alliance with Sparta.

The Boeotian and Corinthian envoys returned home, meeting first with messengers from Argos. Communications were opened between these three and other states on the Spartan proposals and other matters. But coldness and delay set in, and nothing was resolved.

All this was taking place while Athenian-Spartan negotiations continued. Thus ended the eleventh year of the war.

Early in the summer of 420 B.C. the Boeotians failed to send ambassadors to Argos, and made public their alliance with Sparta. Fearing isolation, Argive diplomats were sent to Sparta to discuss the dormant question of an alliance. The Athenians learned of this and other Spartan activities, and the pro-war faction in that city began to rise. It was led by Alcibiades who, motivated by pride, wanted a new arrangement with Sparta or war if one could not be agreed upon.

Comment

This is the first mention of Alcibiades, who is the key figure in the second half of the book.

Alcibiades then sent an envoy to Argos, telling them to come to Athens as soon as possible, and that he would work for an alliance with them against Sparta.

Upon learning that some Athenians were still interested in the conflict with Sparta, the Argives paid no further attention to the negotiations with the Peloponnesian state. Instead, discussions with Athens were initiated.

The Spartans, fearing a new Athenian alliance against them, sent three envoys-Philocharides, Leon, and Endius-to Athens in an attempt to further consolidate the treaty of friendship. Fearful that they might succeed, Alcibiades promised them that if they would withhold information from the Athenian Assembly, he would return Pylos to Sparta and would settle other matters as well. His plan was simple: Alcibiades would disgrace Nicias, the head of the peace party, by having the Spartan mission fail. Then, while the people reflected on the failure, he would push through the Argive alliance, and then set the stage for a resumption of the war. Despite brave efforts by Nicias, Alcibiades' plan was successful; and an alliance with the Argives, Mantineans, and Eleans was soon concluded.

Despite this, the Spartan-Athenian alliance did not come to an end. In addition, contrary to expectations, Corinth did not join in the Argive alliance, and instead moved closer to Sparta.

The Eleans charged Sparta with truce violations during the Olympic Games of 420 B.C. Sparta denied the charges, and refused to make restitutions as demanded by the Eleans. With this, the Argive-Athenian group managed to exclude Sparta from the Games. The feared war did not materialize, however, as Sparta refused to be provoked into breaking the peace. Meanwhile, the Argives approached Corinth in an attempt to win that city over to their side.

Alcibiades, supported by a joint Athenian-Argive force, marched into the Peloponnesian area in the summer of 419 B.C. He was blocked by Corinth and other states from constructing a fort in the area, an act which would have been a serious breach of the peace.

At the same time, war broke out between Argos and the Epidaurians. Argos provoked the war, the major aim of which was to isolate Corinth and assure her neutrality in any future war against Sparta. Despite some preparation for war, Sparta remained true to the treaty. The Argives destroyed about a third of the Epidaurian territory and returned home. Meanwhile a large Athenian force, led by Alcibiades, marched into the area in an attempt to provoke Sparta into war. Failing in this, they went home.

Comment

Remember, Thucydides was an Athenian himself, though an enemy of Alcibiades. He clearly fixes the blame for disturbances upon his own city at this time.

In the months that followed Alcibiades issued provocation after provocation in his attempt to resume the war. "In the middle of the next summer the Spartans, seeing the Epidaurians, their allies, in distress, and the rest of the Peloponnese either in revolt or disaffected, concluded that it was high time for them to interfere if they wished to stop the progress of the evil, and accordingly with their full force, the Helots included, took the field against Argos, under the command of Agis, son of Archidamus, king of the Spartans." Thus, the path to war was being constructed.

Agis invaded Argolis in 418 B.C. A skillful commander, he eluded a superior Argive force and ravaged that city's allies. The

Corinthians clashed with the Argives, who were soon surrounded by the Spartan army. Argive envoys went to Agis, and tried to talk him out of crushing their force. This plea was made without prior consultation with the people. It was accepted by Agis, who also did not consult the people.

Comment

At this stage, many leaders wanted peace, but the general population clamored for a renewal of the war.

The clash was prevented, and Agis withdrew. In both camps, however, the leaders were sharply criticized.

The Athenians, under Laches and Nicostratus, arrived shortly thereafter. The Argives begged them to leave, the leaders having no desire to break the truce. Alcibiades was furious; the Argives had no right to make a truce, he said, and now that the Athenians had arrived, the fighting should recommence. His arguments were successful, and the allies marched on the Spartan ally, Orchomenos, which fell in a short time. Then the allies had violent disagreements as to the next target in their campaign, after which the Eleans went home in a rage.

Meanwhile, Agis was strongly condemned at home for not fighting the Argives. News of the capture of Orchomenos heightened the criticism, and Spartans called for war. Agis was allowed to keep his command, but ten counselors were attached to his army to assure he wouldn't make any future mistakes.

At this point word arrived that an ally, Tegea, was preparing to go over to the Argives. The Spartans mobilized, and set out to save Tegea.

Upon their arrival, the Spartans discovered the Argives in strong defensive positions before the city. Agis withdrew, hoping to lure the Argives into a trap. The Argive commanders met the night, as both sides planned what would be known as the battle of Mantinea.

Comment

Tegea was located in the territory of Mantinea, an ally of Argos and Athens.

Both sides heard speeches before the battle. The Mantineans were reminded that they were fighting for their country. The Argives were told that victory would gain them their rightful place in Greek affairs "and punish an enemy and neighbor for a thousand wrongs." The Athenians heard arguments that the battle would be defensive in that it would preserve Attica from attack, and offensive in that it would enlarge the Athenian empire. The Spartans, on their part, sang war songs, "well aware that the long training of action was of more saving virtue than any brief verbal exhortation, though never so well delivered."

Agis began maneuvering his forces prior to the battle, which gives Thucydides an excuse for discussing military strategy and tactics once more. The maneuvering is not very effective, but "the Spartans, utterly worsted in respect of skill, showed themselves as superior in point of courage." Although defeated in one part of the field, they rallied in others and won the battle. The Argive force was cut in two, and forced to retreat. Over 1,100 Argive and allied soldiers were killed, against 300 or so Spartans, in this, the greatest battle of the war so far. It might have been expected that this would have destroyed Argos' hopes for glory. "Fortune, it was thought, might have humbled them, but the men themselves were the same as ever."

The Spartans sent envoys to Argos in the winter of 418 B.C., in an attempt to reach a peace. A faction within the city wanted to overthrow the government, form an alliance with Sparta, and thus solidify their positions. Although the discussions went slowly at first since Alcibiades happened to be in town, a peace was finally agreed upon. In addition, a fifty year alliance was signed between Argos and Sparta. The two cities agreed not to receive heralds or ambassadors from Athens until that state left the Peloponnesian area. Then Sparta and Argos sent envoys to other states in an attempt to win their support. The Mantineans, desirous of continuing the Confederacy, gave up once Argos came to terms with Sparta. In the next summer Dium revolted against Athens.

Just as all seemed to be going in favor of Sparta, a revolt took place in Argos which led to the victory of an anti-Spartan force, which immediately made overtures to Athens. After a few brief battles, both sides retired from the field. "And thus the winter ended, and the fifteenth year of the war ended with it.

CHAPTER 17

Alcibiades set sail for Argos in the summer of 417 B.C., and seized the remainder of the pro-Spartan faction. The Athenians also made an expedition against Melos, a Spartan colony. Melos was neutral at first, but when Athens attacked the city, its citizens showed great hostility. The Athenians took up positions around the city. Led by Cleomedes and Tisias, they met with the Melians.

Comment

The Melian expedition, which is the heart of this chapter, is one of the most important parts of the book. In it, Thucydides shows how Athens has disintegrated as a result of the war. Under Pericles, the city stood for justice and abstract ideals of right and wrong. Now, the city is power-hungry, and in effect, states that the ends justify any and all means. "Might makes right" seems to have become their motto, as they lose the spirit of freedom which had made them great in the past. Thucydides believes that this was the greatest tragedy of the war, and the major reason for Athens' defeat. A state is strong only so long as it is true to its basic beliefs. Athens betrays them in the Melian **episode**, and thus suffers greatly. This is the act of pride which is mentioned in the introduction.

The Athenian and Melian envoys meet to discuss the situation. The Athenians speak first, stating that they prefer secret meetings, for open ones lead to interruptions on the part of the people, who want to know all sorts of irrelevant things. They want no speech making, but only an accord.

The Melians respond, protesting that the Athenians are acting as judges while they are actually participants in the discussion. What if they prove to be right? Will the Athenians recognize this?

Stick to the issues, say the Athenians. Unless this is done, the discussions might as well end right there.

The Melians are willing to do this, but defend themselves by stating that in matters as important as the future of their city, they have to expand fully.

We will be brief, say the Athenians. We defeated the Persians, thus demonstrating our right to rule. Your arguments for neutrality are unacceptable. "The strong do what they can and the weak suffer what they must."

Do not be vengeful, say the Melians, for such a position may come back to haunt you in the future, for "your fall would be a signal for the heaviest vengeance and an example for the world to meditate upon."

The Athenians are not worried about the end of their empire. There are risks that come with greatness, and they do not shirk them. They ask the Melians to submit to their rule.

The Melians ask whether Athens would accept Melian neutrality, and are told that such a position was not possible. "Either you are for us or against us," is the unsaid belief of the Athenian envoys.

Such a position is unjust, is the Melian retort. In addition, "how can you avoid making enemies of all existing neutrals who shall look at our case and conclude from it that one day or another you will attack them? And what is this but to make greater the enemies that you have already, and to force others to become so who would otherwise never have thought of it?"

We have nothing to fear from states on the mainland, is the Athenian response. As for the prospect of neutrals joining with Sparta as a result of the Melian **episode**, the Athenians reject this.

The Melians reply that if the empire is worth so much to the Athenians, and the envoys admit that they are keeping cities in the empire through force, it would be cowardice to accept such rule. Do the Athenians consider the Melians less brave than themselves?

"Not if you are well advised," is the response. "The contest is not an equal one." It is a question of self-preservation for Melos, and not honor.

The Melians answer that such is not an honorable choice for free men.

"Hope, danger's comforter, may be indulged in by those who have abundant resources," which Melos lacks. Do not be fools, is the Athenian response. Submit or die. The Gods are on our side, since we are strong.

The Melians answer that they are aware of the disproportionate strength of Athens and Melos, but, like the Athenians, they hope the Gods are on their side. In addition, Sparta will come to their aid if attacked. "Our confidence, therefore, after all is not so utterly irrational."

Comment

Having failed to sway the Athenians through an appeal to freedom and liberty, the Melians resort to the Spartan alliance.

"As far as the Gods are concerned," say the Athenians, "we have no fear and no reason to fear that we shall be at a disadvantage." As for the Spartans, they can be counted upon only when their own self-interest is involved. Such is not the case at Melos.

The Melians disagree, stating that Sparta knows that unless she comes to her aid, no other state will trust her in the future.

The Athenian response is short. "Then you do not adopt the view that expediency goes with security, while justice and honor cannot be followed without danger; and danger the Spartans generally court as little as possible."

"Our nearness to Peloponnese makes it easier for them to act, and our common blood insures our fidelity," is the reply.

The Athenians dismiss this too. Submit, they conclude, and do not feel that by accepting us you are committing a dishonorable act. It is not disgraceful to surrender to the most powerful state in all Greece.

With this, the Athenians withdrew, and the Melians were left to consider their fate. After a short deliberation, the Melians told the Athenians that they decided not to surrender. To do so would be dishonorable. They made a last plea for neutrality in the war.

The Athenians refused to consider neutrality, and attacked Melos. After a long siege, the city surrendered. The men of the city were put to death, while the women and children were sold into slavery. Then Athenian colonizers were sent to take over the city.

PELOPONNESIAN WAR

TEXTUAL ANALYSIS

BOOK 6

CHAPTER 18

"The same winter the Athenians resolved to sail again to Sicily, with a greater armament than that under Laches and Eurymedon, and, if possible, to conquer the island; most of them being ignorant of its size and of the number of its inhabitants." Thus, the Athenians embarked on a new aggressive policy of imperialism. The object was to take Sicily, endanger the Peloponnesian allies, and cut Sparta from aid.

After tracing the history of Sicily, Thucydides went into the nature of the expedition. Envoys from Egesta had asked Athens for aid. They were at war with the Selinuntines, who were supported by Syracuse, Athens' enemy. If the Selinuntines won, said the Egestaeans, all Sicily would fall to the Peloponnesians. The Athenians were impressed with these arguments, and decided to aid Egesta.

The Spartans and their allies (except Corinth) marched into Argive territory in the winter of 415 B.C. An Athenian force joined the Argives and razed a small Spartan outpost.

Shortly thereafter the Athenian Assembly voted to send Alcibiades to Sicily to lead the expedition. Nicias, leader of the peace party, was also chosen as a commander, much against his will. He spoke to the Assembly, hoping to divert it from the mission.

Why should we be persuaded by foreigners, he asked, when Athenian blood and treasure is at stake? Affairs at home are critical. Nicias trusts in the Spartan alliance, but should Athens be weakened due to foreign adventures, might not Sparta take advantage of the situation by attacking? In addition, some of Athens' other foreign commitments had not been liquidated. What of the war against the Chalcidians? They had yet to be subdued. In the light of all this, Nicias urges that the expedition not be sent. Finally, he asks what Athens hopes to gain from it, even if the city is successful in taking Sicily. The island is far off, unknown, and difficult to defend. Thus, victory might be worse than defeat.

If all this is true, asks Nicias, why are some Athenians seeking war in Sicily? Referring to Alcibiades, he charges ambition, egotism, and arrogance as being the major causes, and not the future of Athens.

Alcibiades then rose to answer the arguments and charges. He begins by stating that above all others, he has the right to command the armies. He has risked life and fortune in the Olympic Games and on other occasions, when he showed that Athens' greatness was all he desired. As for Sicily, "the cities are peopled by motley rabbles, and easily change their institutions and adopt new ones in their stead; and consequently the inhabitants, being without any feeling of patriotism, are not provided with arms for their persons, and have not regularly established themselves on the land; every man thinks that either by fair words or by party strife he can obtain something at the public expense, and then in the case of **catastrophe** settle in some foreign lands, and makes his preparations accordingly." Why worry about such a mob?

Next, Alcibiades answers Nicias' charges regarding the feasibility of holding Sicily. The Medes were taken with less force, and they were far more powerful than the Sicilians. We cannot set a fixed limit to our empire; if we do, it will be the beginning of our end, for a city is strong only when its visions are limitless. Nothing is so fatal as inaction, says Alcibiades, as he urges the attack.

Nicias spoke again, hoping that new arguments would sway the Athenians. He observes that Sicilian cities are stronger than is commonly thought. In addition, they are provisioned from home, while we have to import food, and they have far more horses than us. All we have, says Nicias, is a weak naval force and an inadequate army. Larger preparations will be needed, he says, in a hope to delay the expedition. If such is not done, he will resign his command.

Nicias was outvoted; Athens wanted the expedition, and told him so in no uncertain terms. As far as the preparations were concerned, they disposed of them by voting large appropriations and giving a completely free hand to the generals. Nicias did not carry out his threat to resign, but reluctantly went along with the rest.

The expedition was about to leave, when it was discovered that the stone Hermae, religious symbols of fertility and prosperity, had been mutilated. "It was thought to be ominous for the expedition, and part of a conspiracy to bring about a revolution and to upset the democracy." Alcibiades had been implicated in such actions during one of his drunken revels, and was charged with acts of impiety. He offered to stand trial, protested his innocence, and offered to die if found guilty. His enemies withdrew, however, and Alcibiades was permitted to sail.

A colorful assemblage was gathered at Piraeus, the port of Athens, as the city came down to bid the expedition good luck and farewell. Then the expedition set out for Corcyra, where the allied forces awaited the Athenian fleet.

CHAPTER 19

Reports of the expedition reached Syracuse, and an assembly was called to discuss the problems caused by the Athenian expedition to Sicily.

The first to speak was Hermocrates. He does not claim to have any special or secret knowledge, but wants his views heard nonetheless.

The Athenians say they want to aid the Egestaeans, but actually, they are out to conquer Sicily, and above all, Syracuse. The city and the rest of the island are well-armed, and will be able to inflict severe casualties on the invaders. As for the Athenian defeat of the Medes, Hermocrates credits that to accidents and luck. Prepare for the attack, he says, and ask for aid from such places as Carthage, but take courage; Sicily will win in the end. Hermocrates also urges a Spartan and Corinthian alliance for safety's sake.

As for the battle itself, Hermocrates feels that there would be great advantage in meeting the enemy at sea. This will prevent the Athenians from gaining provisions before the battle. They will be tired after the long sea voyage. In addition, such an early attack will prevent them from gaining intelligence regarding the Sicilian preparations and resolutions. The courage and bravery of the defenders will surely cause them to retreat.

But few actually believed the Athenians would attack, and thus Hermocrates' speech fell on many deaf ears. Then Athenagoras, a popular leader, rose to speak.

Athenagoras treats the reports of Athens' expedition with scorn. Why should Athens desire a Sicilian campaign? "Now it is not likely that they would leave the Peloponnesians behind them, and before they have well ended the war in Greece wantonly come in quest of a new war quite as arduous, in Sicily; indeed, in my judgment they are only too glad that we do not go and attack them, being so many, and so great cities as we." If they came, the defenders would destroy them in short order. Then Athenagoras launched into a defense of democracy, and rebukes the oligarchs who are inciting the people, in a vain hope of seizing still more power.

At this point, one of the generals steps up and asks for an end to the bickering. More information will be gathered, at which time a proper choice can be made. With this, the Syracusans left the meeting.

Meanwhile, the Athenian expedition arrived at Corcyra, and the forces were joined. Then an expedition was sent to Italy to determine the lay of the land, and which cities they could count on for aid. After this, the expedition set sail.

By the time the fleet reached Sicily, it was clear that there were fundamental differences of opinion between Alcibiades, Nicias, and Lamachus, the third general of the expedition. Nicias wanted to sail to Selinus, which was the main objective of the expedition. Aid would be granted the Egestaeans only if they provided the funds necessary for the voyages. Alcibiades had more ambitious plans. "A great expedition like the present must not disgrace itself by going away without having done anything; heralds must be sent to all the cities except Selinus and Syracuse, and efforts be made to make some of the Sices revolt from the Syracusans, and to obtain the friendship of others, in order to have corn and troops." Thus, Alcibiades' major goal was the capture of all Sicily, with Syracuse as the key objective. Lamachus agreed with the ends of Alcibiades, but disagreed as to means. Why not capture Syracuse immediately? The city was unprepared, and the Athenians could probably win. If they did, all of Sicily would fall soon after.

After speaking his peace, Lamachus agreed to back Alcibiades' proposal, thus outvoting Nicias. Alcibiades then set sail for Messina, with an offer of alliance. He was rejected, and forced to go to Naxos, where he picked up provisions. After a few more sorties, he returned to his base.

While the army moved to Catana, a nearby spot, word came from Camarina that if they went to the town, it would go over to the Athenian side. Since Camarina was near Syracuse, the fleet set sail at once. When it arrived, however, the Camarinaeans refused them, stating that their offer referred to only a single vessel, and not the entire fleet. After destroying some territory belonging to Syracuse, the force withdrew.

Upon their return, the fleet met the Athenian state trireme (a ship), which had orders to bring Alcibiades to Athens for trial.

It seemed that the matter of the Hermae had not ended, and fresh evidence indicated complicity on the part of Alcibiades.

Comment

At this point, Thucydides digresses, and writes of the overthrow of the tyranny of Athens. This created an atmosphere of suspicion, which led to the new accusations. The author indicates that the matter of the Hermae may have been a smokescreen used by Alcibiades' enemies as a means of getting rid of him.

Alcibiades left with the ship, but disappeared at Thurii. Thus, he deserted his city. He traveled to the Peloponnese, and offered his services to Sparta. Alcibiades was then tried in absentia, and sentenced to death.

CHAPTER 20

Nicias and Lamachus divided their forces after Alcibiades left and, now following Nicias' suggestion, sailed for Selinus and Egesta, "wishing to know whether the Egestaeans would give the money, and to look into the question of Selinus and ascertain the state of the quarrel between her and Egesta." The expedition was conducted with timidity, and the rest of the summer saw only brief and inconclusive skirmishes.

The Athenians prepared to march on Syracuse at the end of the summer. The attack was a dismal failure, and the Athenians were obliged to regroup for a more forceful assault. After some maneuvering, the armies were in place. Nicias then spoke to his troops before the battle.

As was usual by then, he began by saying that actions speak louder than words, and that he will therefore be brief. Look around you, he says. Have you ever seen so strong and unified a force? Victory will surely be ours. He closes with this: "I put before you a motive just the reverse of what the enemy are appealing to; their cry being they shall fight for their country, mine that we shall fight for a country that is not ours, where we must conquer or hardly get away, as we shall have their horse upon us in great numbers. Remember, therefore, your renown, and go boldly against the enemy, thinking the present strait and necessity more terrible than they."

Then the battle commenced. The Syracusans fought well, and were not lacking in courage, but they were defeated by the Athenians and their allies. Soon after, the invaders sailed to Naxos and Catana, where they would spend the winter of 415 B.C.

Meanwhile, the Syracusans burned their dead and held a meeting. Once more, the city was addressed by Hermocrates. He tells his countrymen not to lose hope; as long as their spirit holds, they have not been defeated. In addition, the defeat was not as bad as many seemed to believe, and was due to poor generalmanship and unpreparedness. These faults will be shortly corrected. The Syracusans listened to him, and elected Hermocrates himself, Heraclides, and Sicanus as the city's generals. In addition, envoys went sent to Corinth and Spartan to seek aid.

At this point the Athenians sailed for Messina. The plan to take the city was foiled, as Alcibiades, now fighting for the Spartans, told the Messenians of the invasion. Dispirited, the Athenians returned to Naxos.

Learning that the Athenians planned to approach Camarina with an offer of alliance, Hermocrates went to that city to keep it in line. He was permitted to address the Assembly.

He tells the Camarinaeans that he does not fear their acceptance of an Athenian alliance, for he feels sure they recognize it for what it is: an empty gesture not to be trusted. The Athenians love to play the game of divide and conquer; they enjoy accusing some enemy falsely and then attacking on the pretext of defense. And as for this business of Athens having fought Persia to defend Greece from slavery, this too is false. In actuality, Athens and Persia were fighting to determine which state would conquer the rest of Greece. Having defeated the Persians, the Athenians are now trying to enslave us all. All Greece must unite against this danger.

Hermocrates dismisses those who fear the growth of Syracusan power. We do not want to control you, he says, but merely hope to defend Sicily against the invaders. Once the menace disappears, Syracuse can be expected to withdraw. In the meantime, however, the strongest union possible is needed. Neutrality cannot be accepted, for it would, under present conditions, be masked assistance to Athens. In addition, the Spartans should be called in to help. Woe to those who refuse to help defeat the invaders, for if Athens wins, they will not be rewarded. "If the Athenians reduce us, they will owe their victory to your decision, but in their own name will reap the honor, and will receive as the prize of their triumph the very men who enabled them to gain it."

After the speech of Hermocrates, the Assembly heard Euphemus, the Athenian ambassador.

The attacks of Hermocrates lead him to defend Athens and her empire, says Euphemus. Hermocrates stated that Ionians are the eternal enemies of the Dorians; this is correct, but Hermocrates does not say why. "The Peloponnesian Dorians being our superiors in numbers and next neighbors, we Ionians looked out for the best means of escaping their domination." Hence, Athens led an Ionian group for defensive reasons after the Persian Wars. The empire is defensive also, for without it Sparta would rule Greece. We do not make pretentions at being the only city to have fought the Persians, says Euphemus, and our right to rule is not based on this. Athenians are in Sicily, he says, because the safety of Athens demands it. Only enemies need fear enslavement; none of Athens' allies has ever been molested by interference in internal affairs. Our interest in Sicily is not to weaken friends; such a course would be ridiculous. Instead, Athens is only trying to prevent a Syracusan takeover of the entire island. "Any other view of the case is condemned by the facts." Do the Camarinaeans really believe they have more to fear from distant Athens than nearby Syracuse? "We assert that we are rulers in Greece in order not to be subjects; liberators in Sicily that we may not be harmed by the Sicilians; that we are compelled to interfere in many things, because we have many things to guard against, and that now, as before, we are come as allies to those of you who suffer wrong in this island, not without invitation but upon invitation." Euphemus closes by urging the Camarinaeans not to reject the security offered by Athens.

The Camarinaeans sympathized with Athens, and feared nearby Syracuse. As a result, a deadlock developed, and Camarina decided to remain neutral.

While Syracuse continued her preparations for war, Athens tried to gain the confidence and alliance of as many Sicilians as possible. Athenian forces marched on those who refused to join with them and forced some to accept her offer of alliance.

Meanwhile, Syracuse sent envoys to Corinth and Sparta, and they asked for aid against the Athenian force. Corinth agreed to assist, and sent envoys to join the Syracusans in their plea to Sparta. At this point, Alcibiades addressed the Spartans, urging them to fight Athens.

Comment

The following is considered by some writers to be the most brilliant speech in the work, with the exception of Pericles' funeral oration.

First Alcibiades tries to convince the Spartans that their suspicion of him, based on his Athenian background and treachery, is unfounded. He was always friendly to Sparta, he claims, thus ignoring his past warlike statements against that state. What did Sparta do to repay this friendship? Instead of approaching him, her envoys preferred to deal with his political enemies in Athens. Thus, his party was discredited by the very men he had hoped to work with. Because of this, Sparta had no right to complain when he urged an alliance with Argos and the Mantineans, and committed other acts against Sparta. Later on he opposed pro-Spartan tyrants, and Alcibiades readily admits this. But his opposition was not based on a dislike for their foreign policy, but rather on internal politics which had nothing to do with Sparta. "So much then for the prejudices with which I am regarded."

Next, Alcibiades turns to the question of his leadership of the Athenian expedition. He says that the expedition was aimed at taking over all of Sicily, later attacking Carthage, and finally destroying Sparta. (This was not so, but Alcibiades was not that interested in the facts by this time.) The states in Sicily will fall unless Sparta comes to their assistance. If they are taken by Athens, can the destruction of Sparta herself be far behind? Alcibiades urges open and complete aid to Syracuse, which will save that city, serve notice to Athens that she cannot do what she wills in Sicily, and save Sparta herself. He tells the assembly to fortify Decelea and use it as a base for operations against the Athenian army.

What does Alcibiades hope to gain from a Spartan victory? Alcibiades says he loves his country, and is helping Sparta out of a desire to aid his motherland, which was under the yoke of its enemies. He hopes the wars will end with Sparta the strongest power in Greece, and all states free under her benevolent power.

The Spartans accept Alcibiades' advice, and fortify those points which he considered important. Gylippus, a general, is sent to Syracuse at the head of a Spartan force. With this, the events of that, the seventeenth year of the war, ended.

During the summer of 414 B.C. the Athenian force in Sicily was reinforced. Meanwhile, the Spartans marched against Argosppp, and captured much territory before being forced to return due to an earthquake. Soon after, an Argive army attacked Spartan lands, taking captives and land.

The Syracusans learned of Athenian reinforcements, and put off their attack accordingly. But Hermocrates selected a small group for a surprise march on the Athenian position. The Syracusan attack, which took place at Epipolae, was a failure, and on the following day an Athenian force began the attack on Syracuse itself.

Both sides began to construct walls and fortifications outside the city. The Athenians were able to capture some Syracusan positions in the early fighting, although they managed to kill Lamachus in the battle. Nicias, then in sole command, pressed the attack to the point where the Syracusans began proposing terms of peace. But any chance of an Athenian victory of major proportions was lost when Nicias, sick at the time, committed a series of blunders. The most important of these was the permitting of Peloponnesean ships, led by Gylippus, to land in Sicily with reinforcements. "Nicias heard of his approach, but, like the Thurians, despised the scanty number of his ships, and set down piracy as the only probable object of the voyage, and so took no precautions for the present."

About the same time, the Spartans invaded Argos and laid waste to the countryside. An Athenian force relieved the Argives, thus breaking their treaty with Sparta. In the past Athenian aid had been indirect; now, for the first time since the truce, Athenian fought Spartan once more.

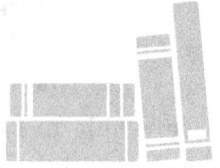

PELOPONNESIAN WAR

TEXTUAL ANALYSIS

BOOKS 7 AND 8

BOOK SEVEN

CHAPTER 21

Gylippus, learning that Syracuse was not completely taken, decided to approach the city by way of Epipolae and then reinforce it. He landed first at Himera, and induced the citizens of that city to join him in the attack. Meanwhile, a Corinthian fleet under the leadership of Gongylus landed at Syracuse. He told the citizens that Gylippus was on his way to help them, and they took courage. The Athenians learned of Gylippus' approach, and prepared to do battle. The Spartan commander sent envoys to the Athenians, offering them a truce if they would evacuate Sicily within five days. The Athenians had nothing but contempt for such a proposal, and did not even answer it. Accordingly, both sides prepared for battle.

The Spartans and their allies won several victories in the early stages of the fighting, forcing Nicias to retreat all along the line. The Athenians reinforced their walls and regrouped. Then followed a series of skirmishes and constructions of walls, in which each side tried to outwit the other. Syracusan and Corinthian envoys were sent to Sparta to ask for more troops, with which they would be able to destroy the last remnants of the Athenian force.

Nicias perceived this, and sent envoys to Athens for reinforcements. The envoys reached Athens in the winter of 414 B.C., and delivered Nicias' letter to the assembly.

The letter opens with a statement regarding the past accomplishments of the army. Nicias observes that it had won many battles until the coming of Gylippus' superior force. Even then, the Athenians won the first encounter, but were soon forced to take defensive positions. Now he was pinned in, while the enemy prepared to attack by sea. The Athenian fleet is in sad shape, and in no condition to resist. Nicias asks for more troops. If they are not sent, then he asks permission to return. In addition, he would like to be relieved of his command, for he suffers from a disease of the kidneys.

The Athenians were not ready to abandon the Syracusan positions. They voted overwhelmingly for large reinforcements, and named Menander and Euthydemus as temporary generals to fill the places of Nicias' dead colleagues. The permanent colleagues, Demosthenes and Eurymedon, were to be sent along with the new army. The Athenians also voted for a new fleet, which would be sent to the Peloponnesian area to prevent a Corinthian or Spartan force from reinforcing Gylippus.

Meanwhile, the Spartans planned an invasion of Athens, in the hope of weakening that city by the presentment of a two front war. The invasion force, led by Agis, set off in the spring.

Decelea, a town some thirteen miles from Athens, was taken and fortified. At the same time a second force, this one of Sparta and her allies and led by Eccritus, set out for Sicily.

The Athenians were not idle in this period. They sent Charicles, at the head of a fleet of thirty ships, to the Peloponnesian area, and further instructed him to call on Argos for reinforcements. At the same time Demosthenes took his large force to Sicily.

Gylippus decided that the best way to stop the Athenians would be on the sea. He was supported in this by Hermocrates, who said that the Syracusans should not be fearful of Athens' supposed prowess on the sea, since this reputation was largely undeserved. The first attacks were unsuccessful, but the skirmishes continued. Finally, the Athenians were defeated.

Meanwhile, Demosthenes was on his way to Sicily with the reinforcements. In addition, a large force of Thracian swordsmen arrived at Athens. They were sent home, however, since the city did not want to pay their salaries.

Comment

A few months before, the Athenians were willing to vote huge appropriations for the Sicilian campaign. The refusal of the Thracian warriors was a sign that the invasion of Agis was having an effect on Athenian morale and finances.

On the way home, the Thracians, who were semi-barbarians, took the town of Mycalessus, destroyed it, and ruthlessly butchered its inhabitants. In particular, they killed the children at a boys' school.

News of the massacre reached Thebes, which quickly outfitted a force to overtake the Thracians and disperse them. This was done, and the Thracians themselves were butchered without mercy.

Comment

In this way, Thucydides dramatizes the growing inhumanity of the war.

Meanwhile, Demosthenes continued on his way to Sicily, and word of his advance proceeded him. Some Sicilian cities which had previously been neutral joined Syracuse at this juncture, in fear of the Athenian invaders.

At the same time a sea fight occurred in the Gulf of Corinth. The battle ended in a draw, although Athens claimed a victory.

As Demosthenes drew nearer, the Syracusans fortified themselves, and in addition made some structural changes in their warships. Rams were added to the ships so as to enable them to crush the Athenian force. The changes proved successful. Together with the superior tactics of Gylippus, the rams were able to defeat the Athenian force. This victory led the Syracusans to believe that they would have no trouble in conquering Demosthenes' army once it arrived.

CHAPTER 22

"In the meantime, while the Syracusans were preparing for a second attack on both elements, Demosthenes and Eurymedon arrived with the succors from Athens, consisting of about seventy-three ships, including the foreigners; nearly five thousand heavy infantry, Athenian and allied; a large number of darters, Hellenic and barbarian, and slingers and archers upon a corresponding scale." The Syracusans were undismayed, for they were reinforced by an equal army and navy.

Comment

This was the largest array of forces in the war.

Demosthenes was convinced that the dallying tactics of Nicias had been wrong, and immediately prepared to attack. At first he layed the surrounding area waste. Then he tried to take some of the Syracusan fortifications, but failed in this. He next attacked nearby Epipolae, but was repulsed by Gylippus and the Syracusans, who were aided by the darkness and disorder. The defenders gained confidence with their victory, and sent to other cities for aid in completely expelling Demosthenes and his army. The Athenians were disgusted with the defeat and at the same time had to fight a small epidemic which had broken out among the troops. Demosthenes urged a withdrawal, but Nicias, previously in favor of such a move, changed his mind and argued for remaining. The Athenians would win, he said, if they could continue to siege. In addition, there was a peace party in Syracuse which might come to their aid. To return would be dishonor, and Nicias felt that death was better than that. Eurymedon agreed with him, and the Athenians did not withdraw.

CHAPTER 23

While the Athenians waited, Gylippus arrived at Syracuse, along with a large army. This alarmed even Nicias, who now agreed to leave for Athens. Preparations for the move were halted, however, when an eclipse of the moon took place. The soldiers, regarding this as a bad omen, prevailed upon their generals to remain, "and Nicias, who was somewhat overaddicted to divination and practices of that kind, refused from that moment even to take the question of departure into consideration, until they had waited the thrice nine days prescribed by the soothsayers."

The Syracusans were overjoyed at this, for they wanted to fight the Athenians and defeat them then and there. A naval engagement followed, during which the Athenians were trounced. The invaders were plunged into a deeper gloom than before, while the Syracusans, their harbor now free, were enthusiastic, and planned to capture the entire Athenian fleet and, in an audacious move, destroy the forces of Nicias and Demosthenes. Eurymedon was killed, and the Syracusans closed the mouth of their harbor with sunken ships, thus forcing the Athenians to stand and fight.

Seeing his soldiers disheartened, weary, and sick, Nicias spoke to them. If you want to see your homes again, he begins, you must fight and win. True, things look bleak, but remember the surprises of war; Athens may yet win in the end. Nicias then outlines the strategy. The navy will lead a retreat, and the soldiers aboard the ships will engage the enemy. Thus, it will be a land battle fought aboard ships. Stay on the ships, he warns, for to land is to die.

Nicias closes by telling his troops that this will be the decisive battle of the war. If they lose, Athens is doomed. "Here you will fall at once into the hands of the Syracusans-I need not remind you of the intentions with which you attacked them - and your countrymen at home will fall into those of the Spartans. Since the fate of both thus hangs upon this single battle now, if ever, stand firm, and remember, each and all, that you who are now going on board are the army and navy of the Athenians, and all that is left of the state and the great name of Athens, in whose defense if any man has any advantage in skill or courage, now is the time for him to show it, and thus serve himself and save all."

Gylippus saw the Athenians going into their ships, and addressed his troops. He reminds them that the Athenians came to Sicily to make them slaves. For the first time, they met their match, and now were on the run. Their morale is crushed, and they will lose the next encounter. Do not think of allowing them to leave, however. Wipe them out now, says Gylippus, and the Athenians will never come again.

Nicias, worried about the coming battle, tried to rally his men again, an action which Thucydides interpreted as weakness. Then, with broken spirits, the Athenians set sail. The fiercest engagement of the war now began. The armies stood aside, as the navies fought it out in a noisy and confused battle. In the end, the Athenian ships broke and ran, and a general panic was set into motion. The army retreated, joining the navy in the loss. Thucydides was unsurpassed in his description of the loss of morale among the Athenians, and the dejection of all who participated. "They had come to enslave others, and were departing in fear of being enslaved themselves; they had sailed out with prayers and paeans, and now started to go back with omens directly contrary; traveling by land instead of sea, and trusting not in their fleet but in their heavy infantry."

Nicias tried to comfort his shattered force. Men had been saved from worse situations, he said. He is physically sick as well as emotionally spent, but still, he had hope. You must be braver now than at any time in the past, he concludes.

But his entreaties are all but useless; the navy, which had refused to sail out, was miserably defeated. The wary Syracusans had blocked the roads, so escape through the land routes was almost impossible. The Syracusan cavalry harassed them whenever they moved, while the supply of food grew shorter and shorter. The Athenians finally gave the Syracusans the slip, but the forces of Nicias and Demosthenes became separated. Demosthenes was quickly surrounded by Gylippus, and after a brief skirmish, was obliged to surrender his six thousand troops.

Meanwhile, Nicias crossed the Erineus river and took the high ground on the other side. He received envoys from Gylippus, who told him of Demosthenes surrender, and demanded the same from the remaining Athenian troops. At first Nicias couldn't believe this, but he was forced to do so when his messengers reported that Demosthenes had indeed fallen. Then Nicias offered to pay the Syracusans and Gylippus a large amount of money, equal to what they had spent on the war, if they would allow his army to leave. This was rejected, and Gylippus attacked fiercely. The slaughter was almost indescribable. "Meanwhile the opposite bank, which was steep, was lined with Syracusans, who showered missiles down upon the Athenians, most of whom were drinking greedily and heaped together in disorder in the hollow bed of the river. The Peloponnesians also came down and butchered them, especially those in the water, which was thus immediately spoiled, but which they went on drinking just the same, mud and all, bloody as it was, most even fighting to have it."

Finally, Nicias had to surrender. He turned himself over to Gylippus, whom he trusted more than he did the Syracusans. Gylippus had hoped to take both Nicias and Demosthenes back to Sparta, where they would participate in his victory parade. But the Syracusans got at them, and they were butchered with other Athenians.

The remaining Athenians were put into a deep quarry, where they were crowded into a small area. "The heat of the sun and the stifling closeness of the air tormented them during the day, and then the nights, which came on autumnal and chilly, made them ill by violence of the change; besides, as they had to do everything themselves in the same place for want of room, and the bodies of those who had died of their wounds or from the variation in the temperature, or from similar causes, were left heaped together one upon another, intolerable stenches arose; while hunger and thirst never ceased to afflict them, each man during eight months having only half a pint of water and a pint of corn given him daily. In short, no single suffering to be apprehended by men thrust into such a place was spared them." Thrucydides estimated that some seven thousand prisoners had been taken. Athenians were sold as slaves. Thucydides concludes the seventh book in this way:

"Thus was the greatest Hellenic achievement of any in this war, or, in my opinion, in Hellenic history; at once most glorious to the victors, and most calamitous to the conquered. They were beaten at all points and altogether; all that they suffered was great; they were destroyed, as the saying is, with a total destruction, their fleet, their army-everything was destroyed, and few out of many returned home."

BOOK EIGHT

CHAPTER 24

News of the disaster was brought to Athens. At first the city was stunned, and for a long while it refused to believe the reports. When the Athenians finally accepted the defeat, they turned on those orators who had urged the Sicilian expedition, "just as if they had not themselves voted it." Next, they began to worry about a Sicilian attack on Athens; many doubted the city could withstand such a blow. Nevertheless, the citizens were determined to defend the city. "In short, as is the way of a democracy, in the panic of the moment they were ready to be as prudent as possible."

While Athens prepared to meet the invasion, all Greece learned of the Sicilian disaster. "Neutrals now felt that even if uninvited they ought no longer to stand aloof from the war, but should volunteer to march against the Athenians, who, as they reflected, would probably have come against them if the Sicilian campaign had succeeded." "Besides, they considered that the war would now be short, and that it would be creditable for them to take part in it."

Comment

Thus, the vultures gather to attack the wounded beast.

The Spartans were overjoyed; a few years before they had feared for their very existence. Now, they planned to take over all Greece. Under Agis, who was king at the time, they gathered a large force for the campaign. Meanwhile, the Athenians were not idle; they too organized an impressive force.

The Athenian preparations were hindered by revolts on the part of her allies. Lesbos, Boeotia, Chios, and other states began talks with Agis on the possibility of their coming over to the Spartan side. Even Tissaphernes, the Persian, made overtures to the Spartans.

At the beginning of the following summer (412 B.C.) the Chians urged an immediate attack, fearing the consequences should Athens learn of their deceptions. A congress was held at Corinth to discuss the matter. A battle plan was drawn up, and was not even kept secret, such was the contempt held by the allies of Athens' power. The attack was held up due to the Isthmian Games, which was attended by Athens.

Comment

Even the war could not stop these games, which were held every four years. During the games, a truce was declared and both sides participated.

The Athenians learned of the attack at the Games, and as soon as they returned home, they took steps to prevent the Spartan fleet from sailing to them, or to Chios. The Athenian attack which followed was successful. Alcamenes, the Spartan commander, was killed, and the fleet was blockaded by the Athenians. The allies were disheartened, but Alcibiades persuaded the leaders to continue the attack. He worked through Endius, an enemy of Agis, for the King was Alcibiades' enemy.

The Athenians met a fleet returning from the Sicilian expedition, and after a brief battle, defeated it. Thus, the tide seemed to be turning in the direction of Athens once more.

Alcibiades and Chalcideus led an expedition to Athens, in an attempt to finally crush that city. An Athenian fleet, led by Strombichides, met Alcibiades, but was forced to flee. Then the Spartans landed in Miletus, and managed to provoke a revolt in that city. As a result, the city was won over from the Athenian side. Immediately thereafter, a treaty was signed between Sparta and Persia, and thus the ancient enemy of Greece entered the war against Athens. The Athenians won a minor victory when a popular revolt at Samos brought that city into the war on their side. Soon after Lesbos was won over as well.

In the same summer an Athenian foray trapped Spartan troops and killed Chalcideus. A victory followed at Chios, and another at Miletus, as Athens counterattacked. A major Athenian victory was prevented when the army was forced to retire on the arrival of Hermocrates and a Syracusan fleet. The Athenians wanted to stay and fight but their commander, Phrynichus, realized that it was no disgrace to retire to fight another day, and so left Miletus.

The Peloponnesian force entered Miletus on the departure of the Athenians, joined with the remainder of Chalcideus' fleet, and attacked and conquered Iasus.

During the following winter the Peloponnesian army solidified its hold on Iasus, while Athens blockaded Miletus and sent a fleet and army to take Chios. Astyochus, the Spartan commander at Chios, failed in several expeditions, and then wanted to set sail for Lesbos, where a new revolution was brewing. His allies prevented this, however, and instead the Peloponnesians went to Miletus.

Comment

The Peloponnesian forces are thus unable to administer the final defeat to the all but destroyed Athenians. At this stage, the war enters a stalemate, during which both sides are bled white.

For the rest of the year the battles seesawed back and forth. Another Peloponnesian fleet was sent to Athens, while an Athenian force besieged Chios. In addition, some Spartans became appalled at the Persian treaty, and demanded its revocation.

CHAPTER 25

The Peloponnesians next decided to sail to Rhodes, hoping to take that island for Sparta. Rhodes, fearful of being destroyed, went over to the Spartans.

Meanwhile, the Spartans began to mistrust Alcibiades, and Astyochus received orders to put him to death. Alcibiades learned of the plot, and fled to the Persian camp and the protection of Tissaphernes. He became an advisor to his new friends, and immediately began to work against Sparta. He sparked dissention in the Peloponnesian camp by spreading rumors that their pay was less than that of the Athenians. "Alcibiades further advised Tissaphernes not to be in too great a hurry to end the war, or to let himself be persuaded to bring up the Phoenician fleet which he was equipping, or to provide pay for more Hellenes, and thus put the power by land and sea into the same hands; but to leave each of the contending powers in possession of one element, thus enabling the king when he found one troublesome to call in the other." Thus, Alcibiades advised the Persians to allow a stalemate to develop, and then step in and take over. After this was done, Alcibiades hoped that he would become, in effect, the puppet ruler of Athens. Alcibiades was correct in his analysis. "When the Athenians at Samos found that he had influence with Tissaphernes, principally of their own motion, the captains and their chief men in the armament at once embraced the idea of subverting the democracy."

Comment

In this way, the path for the destruction of Athenian democracy was charted.

A plot to overthrow the Athenian democracy was organized. Its plan was simple: with the aid of the Persians the democracy would be destroyed, Alcibiades would take over with Persian help, and then reward those who had elevated him. Phrynichus opposed the plot, not so much for love of Athens, but rather because he feared that Alcibiades, his old enemy, would kill him once in power. But Phrynichus was betrayed before he could set a counter-plot into motion.

Then Alcibiades began to work on Tissaphernes, and attempted to convince the Persian of the wisdom of his plan. Meanwhile, his friends arrived at Athens and attempted to sway the citizens to the plan as well. An oligarchy headed by the former traitor, they said, was the only way for the city to be saved.

The Athenians were irritated by this, but agreed that it might be wise to accept a temporary oligarchy, deluding themselves that after a while they could restore the democracy. Phrynichus was dismissed from his post as a prelude to the takeover. This left Alcibiades in a tricky situation. Tissaphernes was following his original plan of playing off one side against the other, while Alcibiades, now on the brink of power, wanted Athens to emerge stronger than before. Agreements were impossible between Athens and the Persians, and the Athenians withdrew from negotiations, convinced that once more they had been deceived by Alcibiades. This was followed by a third treaty between Sparta and Persia, a sign that Alcibiades' plans had fallen through.

Several Spartan victories followed the treaty, as Athens once again had its back to the wall. This gave heart to the oligarchical conspiracy, which once more was set into motion. Those responsible for the banishment of Alcibiades were assassinated, along with others of the democratic camp. The Council was terrorized. "Fear, and the sight of the numbers of the conspirators, closed the mouths of the rest; or if any ventured to rise in opposition, he was presently put to death in some convenient way, and there was neither search for the murderers nor justice to be had against them if suspected; but the people remained motionless, being so thoroughly cowed that men thought themselves lucky to escape violence, even when they held their tongues. An exaggerated belief in the numbers of the conspirators also demoralized the people, rendered helpless by the magnitude of the city, and by their want of intelligence with each other, and being without means of finding out what those numbers really were."

Comment

This is one of the most famous passages in the work. Thucydides reiterates his basic belief that democracies are never destroyed by external challenges, but rather commit suicide through a loss of virtue on the part of its citizens. Even after the Sicilian expedition, Sparta could not conquer Athens. But now, Athens destroys herself.

At this point a force led by Pisander, an ally of Alcibiades', arrived in Athens and assembled the people. First, through a series of ruses, they destroyed the existing government. They met with no opposition. Next, they moved that all power be placed in a Council of 400, to be dominated by them. The proposal was ratified without a single opposing voice. Then a wave of violence began, during which enemies of the new oligarchy were murdered.

Comment

The reader might compare this with the coming to power of Hitler in 1933.

The next step was to send envoys to Sparta to ask for peace. Thinking Athens defenseless, Agis refused them, and planned to take the city by force. The attack failed, and Agis retired from the field. The next Athenian ambassadors were received more kindly, and discussions for a truce were begun.

The oligarchy then sent envoys to Samos, to assure the Athenian army there of the soundness of the new government. But some of the generals, members of the popular party, refused to accept the new government. Plans were made to return to Athens and depose the oligarchs. "The struggle was now between the army trying to force a democracy upon the city and the Four Hundred an oligarchy upon the camp." This came to an end when the Spartan fleet, led by a reluctant Astyochus, sailed to meet the Samian garrison. With this, the Athenians sailed against Miletus, after which they returned to Samos.

CHAPTER 26

The Athenian leaders in Samos decided to invite Alcibiades to be their general, since only he had a chance of winning Tissaphernes over to their side. Alcibiades accepted, making wild promises to the army in the hope of using it to take Athens. The army wanted to sail to Athens at once, but Alcibiades opposed the move. Instead, he set out to meet Tissaphernes, to show the Persian that he was a force to be reckoned with now that he had an army.

Meanwhile, the Peloponnesians were discontent; they already distrusted Tissaphernes, and now that Alcibiades was in control of the Athenian army, they had more reason to do so than ever before. Astyochus, who represented those who wanted to work closely with Persia, was recalled.

At this point the Athenian envoys to Tissaphernes appeared. Had their plans carried through, Athens would surely have passed into Persian hands. Alcibiades did Athens a great service at this point, insisting that the Four Hundred be dismissed and a new government take its place. "Generally he bade them hold out and show a bold face to the enemy." Apparently Alcibiades thought he could gain more power in this fashion than by following the lead of the Four Hundred. Shortly thereafter the government fell, to be replaced by one which comprised the 5,000 wealthiest citizens of the city, who formed a government which was a compromise between oligarchy and democracy. The battles seesawed for a while after this, with neither side gaining an advantage.

The next great battle took place in the Hellespont, where Spartan and Athenian fleets clashed in combat. The Athenians won this engagement, and forced the Spartans to flee. On hearing of this, Tissaphernes set out for the Hellespont with his fleet and troops.

At this point, Thucydides writes: "When the winter after this summer is over the twenty-first year of the war will be completed." This marks the end of his history.

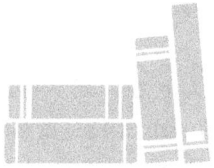

PELOPONNESIAN WAR

CONCLUSION OF THE WAR AND SUMMARY

THE CONCLUSION OF THE WAR AND ITS AFTERMATH

The war continued, with Alcibiades at the head of the Athenian forces. In 410 B.C. the democracy was restored, as Sparta fomented revolt among Athens' allies. In that same year Alcibiades almost completely destroyed the Spartan fleet in the battle of Cyzicus. Once more Athens was in control of the situation. A peace based upon the status quo was offered to Athens, but the radicals in that city, led by Cleophon, rejected it. The war continued.

The following year saw Spartan victories in almost all parts of Greece. Several victories by Alcibiades led Athens to name him general and commander-in-chief in 407 B.C. His moment of glory was short lived, however. In the following year he was defeated by a new Spartan commander, Lysander, and lost his influence in Athens. In 404 B.C. the Athenian fleet was almost wiped out by Lysander near Aegospotami, and the Athenian spirit was broken.

The Peloponnesian army and navy entered the harbor at Piraeus. Thebes and Corinth wanted to raze Athens, but Lysander refused, observing that the city deserved better treatment, if only for her gallantry during the Persian Wars. But the terms set down by Sparta were severe. The walls of Athens were torn down, the overseas possessions were taken from her, and the Athenian fleet was reduced to twelve ships.

From 404 B.C. to 371 B.C. Sparta was the most powerful Greek state. Her ambition, however, led to an alliance of Thebes, Corinth, and the defeated but fast recovering Athens. The leader of the coalition was Thebes, led by Pelopidas and Epaminondas. In 371 B.C. Sparta was defeated by Thebes in the battle of Leuctra, and Thebes assumed the leadership of Greece.

Now, with Thebes as the major Greek power, Athens and Sparta joined forces. Thebes was finally defeated by the allies in the battle of Mantinea (362 B.C.), in which Epaminondas was killed.

For the next few years Greece foundered, while Macedon, a semi-Greek state to the north, grew strong under Philip. In the battle of Chaeronea (338 B.C.), Philip defeated a Greek coalition. He organized a Hellenic League, which included most Greek states but excluded Sparta. Then, as he prepared to lead a unified Greek force against Persia, Philip was assassinated.

With this the city-states rose up, hoping to regain their freedom. But they were put down in short order by Alexander the Great, the son of Philip, the founder of Hellenistic civilization, and the greatest figure of the ancient world.

A SUMMARY OF THE PELOPONNESIAN WAR

Book One. (435-432 B.C.) The book covers the events leading up to the war and its actual beginnings. Athens comes out of the Persian

Wars the most powerful state in Greece. In addition, she has great prestige as the leader of the anti-Persian force. United against her in self-defense are a group of independent states under the leadership of Sparta. Complicating the problem is the fact that Sparta is Dorian and Athens, Ionian. These two people have opposed each other since the beginning of Greek history. In addition, Athens is a democracy while Sparta is controlled by an oligarchy. Finally, Sparta is a land-based power, while Athens relies upon its navy.

Corinth and other pro-Spartan states oppose the spreading of the Athenian empire. Sparta follows this by demanding the breakup of the Athenian empire. Preparations for war are made on both sides.

Book Two. (431-429 B.C.) The war begins, as most Greeks seem to favor Sparta, who proclaims herself the liberator of Greece from the Athenian empire. Athens loses at first, as a mysterious plague sweeps the city. Pericles, the wise and moderate leader of Athens, dies, as the city prepares to sue for peace.

Book Three. (428-426 B.C.) This book deals with affairs in Corcvra and Lesbos, two islands on either extreme of Greece.

Book Four. (425-423 B.C.) After two more years of bitter fighting, a stalemate is reached. A truce is signed in 423 B.C., which neither side takes seriously.

Book Five. (422-416 B.C.) Hostilities are renewed in 422 B.C., but a peace is signed the following year, as Sparta and Athens form a fifty year alliance. For about seven years neither state invades the territory of the other, but each helps its allies and at times invades their territories. The war parties in Athens and Sparta agitate for a renewal of the fighting, as the peace is seen to be unsatisfactory. Athens invades Melos, a neutral state, and destroys it in one of the most inhuman acts of the war.

Book Six. (415-414 B.C.) Athens now attempts to take Sicily, to add that island to her empire. But the expedition is a failure. Alcibiades, the Athenian commander, deserts to the enemy. Nicias, never a brilliant general, is left in command, and fumbles his way from one defeat to another.

Book Seven. (414-413 B.C.) The defending forces under the leadership of Gylippus, defeat and capture the Athenians, who are placed in a concentration camp. The Athenians are now crushed.

Book Eight. (unfinished, 413-411 B.C.) Athens abandons democracy, and undertakes an oligarchic form of government. Alcibiades is recalled from exile, as Athens founders. (Shortly thereafter, the war is ended, with Athens crushed.)

LEADING FIGURES OF THE WAR

Agis

Son of Archidamus, King of Sparta, and later King himself. Agis invaded Attica in 425 B.C. and destroyed the area. He was later forced to flee before Demosthenes. Agis invaded Argolis in 418 B.C. but hesitated after gaining the advantage. He led the forces which defeated Argos in the great battle at Mantinea.

Alcibiades

An Athenian commander who showed great brilliance and audacity. He later deserted to Sparta, and aided that state in its defeat of Athens. Alcibiades plotted to gain control of Athens, and hoped to become tyrant of that city.

Alcidas

A Spartan commander involved in several of the early battles of the war. He fought at Mitylene, and had several victories before fleeing.

Archidamus

A Spartan commander early in the war. He led the first attacks on Athens, despite his friendship with Pericles. Later on Archidamus captured Plataea. He was responsible for winning Lesbos for the Spartan cause.

Athenagoras

A Syracusan, enemy of Hermocrates, who doubted that Athens would attack Sicily in force.

Brasidas

One of the most brilliant and forceful leaders in the book. A Spartan general, he took Megara, Thrace, and other areas in the north. Brasidas subdued Amphipolis and nearly choked the Athenian economy. He was killed near Amphipolis by Cleon's army.

Chalcideus

A Peloponnesian commander who was sent to Ionia with Alcibiades, and helped lead the revolt at Chios, Miletus, and other cities.

Demosthenes

An Athenian commander who attacked Aetolia and failed to take the city. A later expedition under his command captured Delos. Demosthenes was co-commander with Cleon during an attack on Pylos, and afterwards he attempted to stir up revolts in Boeotia. Together with Nicias, he led the Athenians in the ill-fated Sicilian campaign, during which he died.

Diodotus

An enemy of Cleon, who argued for leniency in the case of Mitylene. He won the debate and saved the day for the city.

Eurymedon

An Athenian commander in the campaign against Syracuse.

Gylippus

The brilliant Spartan commander who led the victors in the Sicilian campaign.

Hermocrates

An important leader of Syracuse, who was instrumental in the defeat of Athens in the Sicilian campaign.

Naupactus

An Athenian commander during the Sicilian campaign.

Nicias

A head of the war party in Athens after the death of Cleon. Nicias was Cleon's major enemy, as both tried to take power in the city. He was a rather poor general, who was known for his vacillations. Nicias was in charge of the Sicilian campaign, and he died after Athens' defeat. Before this, he led an attack on Corinth, and took Cythera.

Pericles

An Athenian leader during the early part of the war, and the closest to a "hero" in the book. Pericles was a moderate. He believed that Athens should defend herself through sea power and guard against those who would destroy democracy by arguing that war calls for stricter forms of government. He died in the plague during the first part of the war.

Phormio

An Athenian commander who defeated a Spartan fleet near Acarnania.

Thucydides

The author of the book was a general in the war. He was a general during the attack on Amphipolis, and arrived too late to save the main force. He was later exiled.

Tissaphernes

The Persian leader who subsidized Sparta in the last years of the fighting, and became a leader of the anti-Athenian alliance.

Xenophon

An Athenian commander who captured Potidaea in the early part of the war, and was later defeated at Chalcidice. Xenophon was an historian and wrote of Socrates. It is from his works that we can construct the later history of the war.

STATESMEN AND GENERALS OF THE PELOPONNESIAN WAR

ATHENIAN

Alcibiades, Asopius, Callias, Charicles, Charoeades, Cleomedes, Cleon, Demosthenes, Diodotus, Euphemus, Eurymedon, Euthydemus, Hippocrates, Laches, Lamachus, Menander, Nicias, Nicostratus, Paches, Pericles, Phaeax, Phormio, Phrynichus, Pisander, Strombichides, Themistocles, Thucydides, Tisias, Xenophon

SPARTAN

Agis, Alcamenes, Alcidas, Archidamus, Astyochus, Autocharides, Brasidas, Chalcideus, Cleobulus, Cleomenes, Eccritus, Endius, Epididas, Eurylochus, Gylippus, Leon, Pausanias, Philocharides, Pleistoanax, Ramphias, Salaethus, Sthenelaidas, Xenares

SYRACUSAN

Athenagoras, Heraclides, Hermocrates, Sicanus

PLATAEAN

Astymachus Lacon

BOEOTIAN

Pagondas

CORCYRAN

Peithias

CORINTHIAN

Gongylus

ELEAN

Teutiaplus

PERSIAN

Tissaphernes

THESSALONIAN

Perdiccas

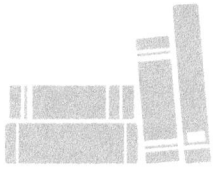

PELOPONNESIAN WAR

ESSAY QUESTIONS AND ANSWERS

Question: How does Thucydides compare with Herodotus as an historian?

Answer: Herodotus, the "father of history," wrote the famous *History of the Persian Wars*. He was a world traveler, and often stories of his journeys crept into his book. Herodotus and Thucydides are considered the greatest of Greek historians, but their works are markedly different. Herodotus relied upon oral evidence far more than Thucydides, and was not as critical of the stories he heard as was the author of the *Peloponnesian War*. In addition, he had little grasp of military strategy, while Thucydides, a general, gives us one of the best descriptions of military life among the Greeks. In Herodotus' work the gods intervene in human affairs, while they do not in the *Peloponnesian War*. Cause and effect are not clear at times in Herodotus, and his speeches, often fabricated as are those of Thucydides, are not nearly as accurate.

On the other hand, it must be remembered that Herodotus blazed the trail, writing as he did when the art of history was still in its infancy. In addition, despite his pro-Greek biases,

Herodotus does try to be impartial, as does Thucydides. Finally, he realized the importance of social and economic factors in history far more than Thucydides.

Question: What is the "lesson" of the *Peloponnesian War*?

Answer: Thucydides tried to show us that the greatest dangers to democratic states are internal rather than external. Athens is strong only so long as she believes in herself, has a moral code which most citizens accept, and is led by moderate men like Pericles. Although suffering military defeats and plague in the early years of the war, she is able to survive due to internal unity.

After the death of Pericles, and with the coming to power of Cleon, these conditions change. In her treatment of both friends and allies, Athens begins to abandon her previous beliefs. This is most vividly shown in the case of Melos. After this Athens has a series of victories but, due to the sin of hybris, is doomed to defeat.

Question: What is the difference between Thucydides and modern historians?

Answer: Although known as an historian, Thucydides is actually more in the tradition of teachers of morality. He apparently began his work in the belief that there were patterns of behavior which emerged during the war, and that they could be repeated in the future.

Most modern historians shy away from this method and philosophy, although they will admit that at times they cannot avoid the sweeping generalization, the moral lesson, and the construction of a structure which ignores or plays down some events while magnifying others. They do this in an apologetic way, however, and excuse themselves by observing that they were men before they became historians.

Ideally, today's historian enters his problem area with as few preconceptions as possible, although with the belief that the problem will be interesting and informative. He then begins to examine the evidence. As he goes along, cause and effect relationships begin to develop, and pieces begin to fit into a jigsaw puzzle he had constructed in his mind's eye. At this point he forms a tentative hypothesis, or belief about the nature of the problem. Then, he tests the hypothesis against the evidence. As he finds facts which do not support it, he changes the hypothesis. At times the weight of these facts may be such that he will abandon the hypothesis for a new one, and then begin all over again. One historian remarked that the research of an historical problem is to be compared to a monkey on a stick, going up and down from hypothesis to evidence, and then all over again, almost endlessly.

After this goes on for some time, the historian decides that he has reached a point of diminishing returns, is fairly content with his hypothesis and, if he is honest with himself, is somewhat tired of the endless research involved in the question. It is at this point that he begins to write.

The final work, when published, is offered not as "the last word" on the subject, but rather as the author's reflections on the evidence he has gone into, and the knowledgeable reader knows that the author's personality, the times in which he lives, his background, ethical conceptions, etc., are as much a part of the work as the evidence. It is for this reason that when a new historian appears, with different values, at a different time and place, a different hypothesis may appear. This goes on endlessly, for the writing of history is an art, and not an exact science.

Of course, this is at variance with what Thucydides thought he was doing. Still, his insights into "human nature" are such as to win the respect of many historians, especially those of the more psychological orientation. This was recognized by such men as Theodore Roosevelt, who carried a pocket edition of the *Peloponnesian War* with him on his African expedition, and by Secretary of State George C. Marshall, who once said, "I doubt seriously whether a man can think with full wisdom and with deep convictions regarding certain of the basic international issues today who has not at least reviewed in his mind the period of the Peloponnesian War and the fall of Athens." And most of our knowledge of this period comes from Thucydides. Like it or not, we see the war through his eyes.

Question: If Thucydides did not complete his book, how do we know about the ending of the war?

Answer: Xenophon of Athens, also a general in the Peloponnesian War, (who was banished from Athens and wrote under Spartan patronage), wrote of the war in the Hellenica. He picks up where Thucydides left off, and describes how Athens fell. Then he goes on to show the failures of Sparta in creating an empire, the rise and fall of Thebes, and the general aftermath of the Peloponnesian War. Unlike Thucydides, Xenophon was not a Sophist, but rather a friend of Socrates. He was a world traveler, and had a great breadth of vision. Xenophon was rather shallow, however, and his work is not in the same category as that of Thucydides.

Question: What was Thucydides' conception of history?

Answer: Thucydides was a mechanist in that he believed that when faced with similar problems, similar people will react in similar fashions. Individuals do not believe this, and attempt to exert their free will in order to change the world. This is vanity, he says; for although one may change immediate situations, the end products of large scale enterprises are the results of mechanical forces present in nature and in man.

This is not to say that Thucydides believed the gods controlled man's destiny; the gods play no role at all in his history. Rather, it is what today we call "human nature" that determines actions. Thus, Thucydides may be viewed as a predecessor of Freud and the social Darwinists of the second half of the nineteenth century. Freud and his later followers believed that our actions are the results of certain forces inborn in man, while the social Darwinists thought that morality, actions, values, etc. are part and parcel of the struggle for existence. Thucydides does not attempt to offer a complete psychological portrait of men like Pericles and Cleon, or Alcibiades and Nicias, but the psychologically-oriented student can see that the faint glimmerings of that discipline can be found in his book.

SELECTED BIBLIOGRAPHY

Burn, A.R. *Pericles and Athens*. New York: The Macmillan Company, 1949. The best single survey of Athens during its Golden Age.

Bury, J.B. *The Ancient Greek Historians*. London: The Macmillan Company, 1909. Old, but the sketch of Thucydides' methodology is still highly regarded.

Cochrane, C.N. *Thucydides and the Science of History*. Oxford: Oxford University Press, 1929. An attempt at placing the historian in the context of his times and the stream of historical thought.

Dickinson, G.L. *The Greek View of Life*. New York: Doubleday, Doran & Co., 1930. A subjective essay on many aspects of Greek thought, including an illuminating discussion of Greek historians.

Finley, J.H. Jr. *Thucydides*. Cambridge: Harvard University Press, 1942. The best work on the subject.

Hamilton, E. *The Great Age of Greek Literature*. New York: W.W. Norton & Co., 1942. Pleasing, with some interesting comparisons to other figures.

Henderson, B.W. *The Great War Between Athens and Sparta*. London: The Macmillan Company, 1927. An extremely detailed study on the war, and on Thucydides' methods of presenting it. Rather tough sledding for the novice.

Rostovtzeff, M. *A History of the Ancient World*. 2 vols. Oxford: Clarendon Press, 1933. Greek history in relation to that of the rest of the ancient world. Especially good on the Peloponnesian War.

Zimmern, A. *The Greek Commonwealth: Politics and Economics in Fifth-Century Athens*. Oxford: Clarendon Press, 1931. A good subjective study of Athens during this period.

www.ingramcontent.com/pod-product-compliance
Lightning Source LLC
LaVergne TN
LVHW011727060526
838200LV00051B/3062